Reading and Interpreting the Works of

JOHN STEINBECK

 Enslow Publishing
101 W. 23rd Street
Suite 240
New York, NY 10011
USA
        enslow.com

Lit Crit
Guides

Reading and Interpreting the Works of

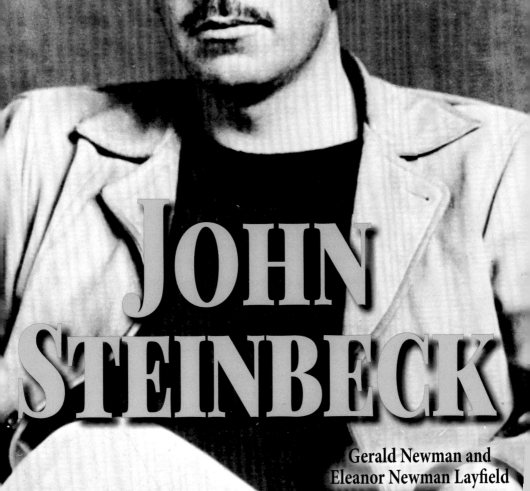

JOHN STEINBECK

Gerald Newman and
Eleanor Newman Layfield

For Juliane Quinn Newman

Published in 2016 by Enslow Publishing, LLC
101 W. 23rd Street, Suite 240, New York, NY 10011

Library of Congress Cataloging-in-Publication Data

Newman, Gerald.
 Reading and interpreting the works of John Steinbeck / Gerald Newman and Eleanor Newman Layfield.
    pages cm. — (Lit crit guides)
 Includes bibliographical references and index.
 ISBN 978-0-7660-7348-7
 1. Steinbeck, John, 1902–1968—Juvenile literature. 2. Steinbeck, John, 1902–1968—Criticism and interpretation. 3. Authors, American—20th century—Biography—Juvenile literature. I. Layfield, Eleanor Newman. II. Title.
 PS3537.T3234Z7768 2016
 813'.52—dc23
 [B]
                    2015029185
Printed in the United States of America

To Our Readers: We have done our best to make sure all website addresses in this book were active and appropriate when we went to press. However, the author and the publisher have no control over and assume no liability for the material available on those websites or on any websites they may link to. Any comments or suggestions can be sent by e-mail to customerservice@enslow.com.

Portions of this book originally appeared in *A Student's Guide to John Steinbeck*.

Photo Credits: Cover, pp. 3, 25, 110 Hulton Archive/Getty Images, vectorgraphics/Shutterstock.com (series logo); p.6 Rolls Press/Popperfoto/Getty Images; p. 9 © AP Images; p. 15 Ken Wolter/Shutterstock.com; p. 20 General Photographic Agency/Hulton Archive/Getty Images; p. 31 J. R. Eyerman/The LIFE Picture Collection/Getty Images; pp. 38, 43 Culture Club/Hulton Archive/Getty Images; p. 49 © Heritage Image Partnership Ltd / Alamy; p. 55 Loomis Dean/The LIFE Picture Collection/Getty Images; p. 62, 68 Everett Historical/Shutterstock.com; p. 73 © World History Archive / Alamy; p. 79 Ruth Peterkin/Shutterstock.com; p. 85 Carol M. Highsmith/Buyenlarge/Getty Images; p. 90 Terry Disney/Express/HUlton Archive/Getty Images; p. 97 ruskpp/Shutterstock.com; pp. 102, 131, 136 © AP Images; p. 115 Evening Standard/Hulton Archive/Getty Images; p. 120 Rolls Press/Popperfoto/Getty Images; p. 126 Keystone/HUlton Archive/Getty Images; p. 138 Jemal Countess/Getty Images Entertainment/Getty Images.

Contents

John Steinbeck

LIVING IN SALINAS

John Steinbeck's best-selling novel, *East of Eden*, is set in Salinas, California, a town with a population of about 2,500, fifteen miles east of Monterey Bay. Salinas was his family's home, the place where he was born on February 27, 1902.

The novel begins:

> The Salinas Valley is . . . a long narrow swale between two ranges of mountains, and the Salinas River winds and twists up the center until it falls at last into Monterey Bay . . .
>
> The Salinas was only a part time river. The summer drove it underground . . .
>
> But there were dry years too, and they put terror on the valley . . . And it never failed that during the dry years the people forgot about the rich years, and during the wet years they lost all memory of the dry years. It was always that way.
>
> And this is about the way the Salinas Valley was when my grandfather brought his wife and settled in the foothills.[1]

Many of Steinbeck's novels and short stories take place in or around this California town. Many of his essays recall his youth there. John's mother, Olive, was an active member of Salinas society. She was a fund raiser who planned community functions for the town. Through Olive's connections, John's father, John Ernst Steinbeck II, was able to become town treasurer, a position he held until his death in 1936. Though the Steinbecks were never really wealthy (at one point John Ernst II went bankrupt), they were financially secure. The Steinbecks were the typical churchgoing family, with three daughters, Beth, Esther, Mary, and one son, John.

Young John

Photos seem to indicate John was not a very good-looking kid.[2] His mother called him "little squirrel"; his sisters nicknamed him "muskrat." The nicknames were meant affectionately, but they were disturbing to John, who was very sensitive about his looks. His ears stuck out, and he was plagued by acne well into his college years. Because John was the only boy, his father expected more from him than he did from his daughters. John took full advantage of his position in the household by often getting into trouble. Mary and older sister Beth took good care of him, but both considered him "spoiled."[3]

In 1908 the Steinbecks enrolled John in the Baby School, the primary school on Central Avenue in Salinas. He was far ahead of his classmates in reading because he had the advantage of being home tutored by his mother.[4] John was a loner, spending much of his free time playing in his backyard or reading in his room. He enjoyed books such as *Alice in Wonderland* and *Tom Brown's Schooldays*, but myths and legends were his favorites, especially Sir Thomas Malory's *Morte D'Arthur*.[5] John's younger sister, Mary, remained John's

John Steinbeck was born in this house in Salinas, California, in 1902.

confidante through most of his adolescence. She took on the role of best friend when he had no friends and shared with him a unique rapport.[6]

A Budding Writer

When he entered Salinas High School in 1915, John Steinbeck remained mostly out of touch with the other students. He never volunteered in class and worked just hard enough to get slightly above-average grades. John hardly dated nor was he invited to parties, and he was rarely part of group activities or events. However, he did get along with a few boys on a one-to-one basis. One friend was Max Wagner, who lived in Mexico before coming to Salinas. Through Max, John became friends with some of the town's Mexican teenagers.

Though his high school yearbook indicates that he was a member of the track, football, and basketball teams, his awkward size and ungainliness attributed to his failure as an athlete. He was also a failure as a member of the student training corps, a volunteer group like Junior ROTC that aided in the war effort. He hated marching around in a uniform, and he hated even more getting up before dawn. However, with a total school population of one hundred students, everyone was expected to participate in some activities. In addition to athletics and the training corps, John also joined the drama society and the science club. He was elected senior class president and associate editor of the yearbook, a position he enjoyed and at which he was successful.[7] A student a year younger than John remarked: "John was known as a writer even then. He would get you in a corner and spin a hell of a yarn. From what people said to me at the time, he wrote a good bit of the yearbook all by himself. It just didn't surprise any of us when he became famous for his books."[8]

In June 1919, just after World War I ended, John graduated from Salinas High School. He was off to Stanford University, happy for a chance to get out of Salinas.

An Off-and-On-Again Student

John agreed to go to college only if he could study writing, much to his parents' dismay. John was enrolled at Stanford University, off and on, from the fall of 1919 to the spring of 1925. He was an English major, concentrating on creative writing. He studied Greek and Latin and participated in the army's ROTC, riding the corps' horses when they were not used for training.

Unfortunately, he also brought his lackadaisical attitude to college. Even worse, he became a poker player and a drinker. Late nights of card games, drinking, and carousing meant missed classes and late assignments. Probation notices constantly followed him. John rarely completed courses, often dropping them in mid-semester. All told, he earned only three years of credit in the six years he was at Stanford. Without Steinbeck's roommate, George Mors, a straitlaced, clean-cut young man who tried to look after him, Steinbeck might not have gotten that far.

The summer after his first year at college, John got a job working in a factory along with Mors. By summer's end, Steinbeck decided he would put off returning to school and continue working instead. He would not return to Stanford until the fall of 1921.

Gathering Notes

When he did return to Stanford, Steinbeck remained on probation. Many of the problems he had before remained unresolved, such as his tendency to spend more time in the library reading material of his own choosing rather than what his professors required.

That Christmas, Steinbeck went to Oakland and stayed with a friend, Robert Bennett. He found a temporary job at Capwell's Department Store, selling men's clothes. Then he got a job as part of a dredging crew to dig a ditch from Salinas to Castroville so that markers could be placed to indicate a canal route. He hated to be doing manual labor again, but he was well-liked by the men he worked with. They taught "Johnny boy," as they called him, to gamble, drink, and smoke marijuana.

On one occasion, Steinbeck offered a group of men money for any stories they could tell him about themselves. A young man named Frank Kilkenny told him about a kind farmwife who nursed him with her breastmilk when he was on the brink of starvation. Steinbeck was so moved by the story that he gave Kilkenny two dollars, a large sum of money in 1922.

Steinbeck then worked at a ranch as a foreman of Mexican and Filipino workers who hauled heavy bags of beets onto trucks. In the evenings he would sit with his men and listen to them talk about their lives. He knew that to be successful at this job, the men—tough, illiterate vagabonds—had to respect him, so he worked much harder than they did. After four months he quit and returned to his parents' home. He read all day and drank all night with no clue as to why his writing was not what he wanted it to be. At his father's insistence, he even sought psychological help from a family doctor who thought John's problem was caused by a low-grade viral infection. Then one night, as he scrawled on his pad, he realized that he had accumulated all these notes about the people he had met: the downtrodden, penniless underclass he so respected and admired.

Influences

Steinbeck returned to Stanford in the winter of 1923, believing that this time he was more mature, more determined to actually become a writer, more aware of who he really was. This time his grades were A's and B's. At registration he ran into a classmate, Carlton Sheffield, known as "Dook," whom he had met in French class when they were freshmen. Because the two found common ground in being English majors, hoping to become professional writers, and having a strange sense of humor, they quickly became roommates and close friends.

Well aware of class and race distinctions on campus, Steinbeck did what he could to thumb his nose at those distinctions. One time he brought a Chinese date to the prom, which shocked both the students and the faculty. On another

STEINBECK'S CONTEMPORARIES: F. SCOTT FITZGERALD

Born six years after Steinbeck, Francis Scott Key Fitzgerald wrote *This Side of Paradise*, his first novel, in 1920. It's about being rich, young and famous. As author of this roaring twenties novel, Fitzgerald is credited with originating the "flapper," a young woman whose entire existence is about living high on life and low on morals.

But it was *The Great Gatsby* (1925), Fitzgerald's third book, which became an American classic. As told by Tom Buchanan, it is the story of Jay Gatsby, a young millionaire who has accrued his wealth through bootlegging and racketeering. The story, itself, is actually told by Tom Buchanan, the husband of Daisy, Gatsby's beautiful, but shallow mistress.

Fitzgerald died of a heart attack in 1944.

occasion he decided to challenge the policy of not allowing drinking on campus. He sat down in front of a palm tree near the Memorial Church on the Inner Quad, a gallon of red wine in tow, and spent the night drinking. In addition, he had altered the carillon in the church to play "How Dry I Am," a drinking song. The dean was not amused.

Steinbeck became a driving force in the English Club, not only because he was constantly writing and needed a forum to present his work, but also because it earned him acknowledgment by members of the faculty.

Edith Ronald Mirrielees, a short-story writing teacher, was Steinbeck's greatest influence at Stanford. She forced him to say what he meant rather than allow him to overwrite. She forced him to make revisions, which he often resisted. She made him write clearly, simply, and succinctly. In short, she helped to turn him into a professional. He became her top student of all time. She rewarded him with a grade of B, which annoyed Steinbeck, but he understood it was given so that he would continue to work harder.[9] Years later she occasionally spoke about Steinbeck in her class. Her only negative comment was that he was too sentimental even in his later works. She said she wished he had eliminated the last few paragraphs of *Of Mice and Men*.[10]

During the summer of 1924, Steinbeck and his friend Dook returned to Salinas. After working for a few months on the night shift at the factory, Steinbeck took a final turn at Stanford. This time, however, he avoided the dorm and instead rented a toolshed attached to a barn behind a house on Palo Alto Avenue. It had no electricity, no gas, and no water. He cleared a living area about six feet square where he placed an army cot, a wooden box that held an old Corona typewriter, and an assemblage of gallon jugs for the wine he

When Steinbeck wasn't attending classes at Stanford he often returned to Salinas. His hometown would play an important role in much of his writing.

planned to make. He paid five dollars to rent the home he called "The Sphincter." The room was alternately dubbed "The Den of Pegasus." Invoking the image of the mythical flying horse was meant to represent the fantastical dreams of John and his fellow writers. He later decided that it should not be a flying horse, but a flying pig, which he dubbed "Pigagus": "a lumbering soul but trying to fly," with "not enough wing-spread but plenty of intention."[11]

One reason Steinbeck chose to live in seclusion was so he could concentrate on writing without being disturbed by outside influences. He also began making wine at home. John befriended fellow English Club member Elizabeth Smith, who went by the pen name John Breck. The two threw many parties at her house. Dook Sheffield realized the importance of John's relationship with Breck: "This is John's real university. Everything was up for *discussion*: music, books, politics. I think everyone was surprised by how knowledgeable John was. It would have surprised most of his professors."[12]

Steinbeck's writing was going well. He had completed several stories, some of which even he thought were good. He showed one of them, "A Lady in Infra-Red," to Breck, who immediately recognized it as autobiographical. Breck saw the faults in the story but convinced John to expand it into a full-length novel. Steinbeck expanded the story into an allegory about a poor Welsh boy who runs off to the Caribbean to find his fortune. But when he has no luck and becomes a pirate, he is forever banished from returning home. By May he had completed forty pages, which Breck's daughter Polly typed for him. But because he spent so much time working on the novel, Stanford again warned him that he was facing suspension since he had missed so many classes.

Living in New York

Steinbeck left Stanford for good in 1925. His father even offered to give him an allowance of twenty dollars a month for six months so that he could complete the novel. Steinbeck went off to the cottage in Pacific Grove to meet the deadline, but the more he wrote the more he hated the book. In October 1925, he took the manuscript to John Breck, who refused to read it because he was angry over his leaving school. He then brought the novel to Edith Mirrielees, who, after reading it, told him to forget it and return to Stanford for more education and experience. But Steinbeck told his father he was not returning to school and he would no longer ask him for support.[13]

Steinbeck decided to go to New York to become a reporter. He eventually settled in his sister Beth's walk-up apartment in the Fort Greene section of Brooklyn. He found a job at a construction company that was building the new Madison Square Garden on Eighth Avenue and Fiftieth Street in Manhattan. After fifteen to eighteen hours a day of hauling wheelbarrows filled with cement up ramps to men high up in the scaffolding, he was exhausted by the time he got back to Brooklyn each night. His sister remembers him eating a sandwich for dinner and then going directly to bed without ever writing a word. It was a job he could not keep. Finally, after seeing a coworker fall from the scaffolding to his death, Steinbeck quit.

allegory
A symbolic representation or expression.

Steinbeck's maternal uncle, Joe Hamilton, got him a position on William Randolph Hearst's *New York American* as a cub reporter. He combed the streets for stories and usually found them, but his reportage suffered from the same problems as his work in college: It was too flowery, too overwritten. He was reassigned to the courts down in the Park Row section of Manhattan where the hardened reporters there could train him. He remembers playing bridge, sharing the liquor given to the reporters by judges who confiscated it because of Prohibition, and becoming a much better reporter. He found it "a happy place to work."[14] With the little money he was now earning, Steinbeck moved into what was then the Parkwood Hotel near Gramercy Park in Manhattan. He lived in a dingy, bug-infested apartment on the sixth floor that cost seven dollars a week. Along with Ted Miller, a friend from Stanford who had also moved to New York, Steinbeck spent nights sampling local restaurants and discovering the city. Sometimes he covered a trial; sometimes he ventured into Brooklyn or Queens to cover a story and wound up getting lost. Eventually, he got fired.

Steinbeck sent some of his stories to Guy Holt, a friend who worked for a small publishing house that took an interest in new writers. Holt liked what he read and promised Steinbeck he would publish a collection of his work if Steinbeck would submit six more stories as good as the first ones. During the next few weeks, Steinbeck worked feverishly to finish the stories. When they were done, Holt was no longer with the company, and the new editor had no interest in publishing the collection of stories. Steinbeck was so enraged that he began shouting and cursing and physically assaulting the editor.[15] Holt's new employer, the John Day Company, was equally uninterested in the short stories. Holt suggested that John go home and write a novel.[16]

A Seven-Dollar Short Story

Steinbeck returned home to San Francisco for the rest of the summer. As a ship's steward he served food, cleaned up, and in his spare time wrote letters for the crewmembers and even beat up the ship's bully. For the rest of the summer he joined Toby Street in Lake Tahoe. Ultimately, Steinbeck spent more time writing to friends to tell them about his loneliness and writer's block than he did writing the novel. In March 1927, with no luck on the novel, he tackled an old short story, "The Gifts of Iban," he had started at Stanford. Once it was rewritten, he sent it off under the pen name John Stern to an obscure magazine called *The Smoker's Companion*. The magazine published it, paid him a royalty of seven dollars, and asked for more stories. He never told his family or friends he had made the sale.[17]

Meeting Carol Henning

By the end of January 1928, Steinbeck's novel was done. The short story "A Lady in Infra-Red" was transformed into the novel *The Pot of Gold*, and then retitled *Cup of Gold*. But Steinbeck hated it. He mailed it to Ted Miller, but Miller returned the manuscript because it was handwritten. Steinbeck needed a stenographer—someone to type up what he had written. He eventually found one, a woman named Carol Henning. She was twenty-two years old and was vacationing with her sister Idell at Lake Tahoe. At first Steinbeck did not think Henning was very pretty, but he admired her personality and forthright attitude.[18] He offered her a nickel a page to type the work, and within days she presented him with a neatly composed manuscript. Henning thought very highly of the novel and could not understand Steinbeck's fears about it. She so enjoyed being part of the manuscript-to-printed-page process that she refused to take any money for her work. Steinbeck was

As a young man in his twenties, Steinbeck lived in San Francisco, writing and doing manual labor.

distraught when she and her sister left. He knew he had to see Carol Henning again.

Soon after, Steinbeck left for San Francisco. His sister Mary's new husband, Bill Decker, whose family owned part of the Bemis Bag company, got him a job in a warehouse hauling heavy bales of jute or hemp on hand trucks. Whenever Steinbeck was not hauling bales of sacks into storage or attempting unsuccessfully to write, he was running around town with Henning, having inexpensive dinners in North Beach or hopping the streetcars to spend a day at the beach.

In October, Steinbeck moved into the top floor of a walk-up on Powell Street. It had the traditional Steinbeck look, complete with mice "scratching all night in the walls and ceilings." As his sister Mary recalled, "He never minded being down-and-out. I think he actually liked it. Young writers were supposed to be poor."[19] The San Francisco experience was a pleasant one, even though it was not financially rewarding. Steinbeck would read chapters to the Henning sisters and, when he was not working, drop in at local discussion groups whose members discussed current happenings. Steinbeck used the few dollars he had left to buy Carol Henning's old Buick and return to Pacific Grove. At least there he could live rent-free and concentrate on writing without having to worry about where the next dollar came from. His father, optimistic that *Cup of Gold* would earn some money, again offered him an allowance until royalties began coming in.

Cup of Gold
Gets Published

*C*up of Gold, a fictional biography of the notorious pirate Henry Morgan, was finished in the fall of 1929. Undoubtedly, Carol Henning was a strong factor in John's newfound enthusiasm for writing. She had suggested he read Ernest Hemingway, who became influential in his writing style, though Steinbeck never admitted it. She believed in Steinbeck perhaps more than he believed in himself. She observed and coached and edited and did everything else she could to help him become the writer he wanted to be.

At last *Cup of Gold* found a publisher. In early 1930, Robert M. McBride and Company agreed to release the book. Even though this was the same publisher that rejected his stories a few years before, Steinbeck decided to go with McBride because it was more enthusiastic than any other publishing company about the possible success of the book. They even contracted Steinbeck's friend Mahlon Blaine to design the dust cover.

When summer arrived, Steinbeck moved to Palo Alto to live with Dook Sheffield and his wife. Dook had returned to Stanford to work on his master's degree. On weekends he and Dook would edit what Steinbeck had written during the week and Henning, who would take the train down from San Francisco, would type the revised pages. In August, Henning used her vacation time to go camping with Steinbeck in the hills of La Honda, near Palo Alto. Each morning Steinbeck would wander off into the woods to a tree stump he used as a desk. He would set out his pens and bottle of ink and devote himself entirely to neatly entering his novel into a ledger.

Cup of Gold was finally published in August 1930. Steinbeck earned a small royalty, enough for him to live comfortably for a short while.

Carol

John Steinbeck and Carol Henning were similar in many ways: Both were bright, stubborn, and independent. They knew how to have fun, laugh at life's absurdities, and though they saw the dark side of almost everything, they could also stand back and dismiss it. Their differences were more important. Much like his father, Steinbeck was quiet, even withdrawn, but still argumentative, while Henning was assertive and funny. He

STEINBECK'S CONTEMPORARIES: ERNEST HEMINGWAY

Born on July 21, 1899, in Oak Park, Illinois, Ernest Hemingway was just three years older than Steinbeck. He died on July 2, 1961, the result of a suicide by gunshot.

Hemingway was known primarily for such works as *The Sun Also Rises* (1916), *A Farewell to Arms* (1929), and *The Old Man and the Sea* (1952), which tells the story of Santiago, an old fisherman who spends eighty-four days at sea waiting for a catch. When he is finally able to harpoon a marlin, he returns to shore only to have his fish attacked by sharks. *The Old Man and the Sea* is a simple, touching tale of courage, friendship, patience, and pride.

Like Steinbeck, Hemingway was a recipient of the Nobel Prize in Literature.

was plagued by mood swings, while she had a steady temperament. He was insecure about his prospects, while she believed he had a profitable and fulfilling future.

Steinbeck and Henning married. They moved in with Dook Sheffield and his wife in their house near Occidental College in Los Angeles and then rented a dump of a house in the same Eagle Rock neighborhood. The rent was a mere fifteen dollars a month.[1] On January 14, 1930, the Sheffields escorted John Steinbeck and Carol Henning to the courthouse in Glendale, where they were married, without ever having told his or her parents or friends about the event.[2] Through it all John Steinbeck continued to write, and by the spring of 1930 *To an Unknown God* was finished. It was based on his maternal grandparents, the Hamiltons, but used the story of his grandfather Steinbeck's migration from New England to California.

It was a happy time for them all. The Steinbecks did not have much money, but John was productive and Carol seemed to be a good influence on his work. In June, they moved to a wood-frame house in Tujunga, not far from Eagle Rock. With the help of John's father, Carol Steinbeck found a job as the secretary to the secretary of the chamber of commerce in Monterey. Steinbeck, who felt both energized and filled with inner peace, began spending about five hours a day writing a new book.

To an Unknown God (the title was revised) could not find a publisher. No one seemed to be interested in a psychological novel about a paranoid individual, especially during the Depression. Steinbeck was disappointed but undaunted. He wrote to Carol: "I have high hopes for myself . . . Eventually I shall be so good that I cannot be ignored. These years are disciplinary for me."[3]

John Steinbeck is seen here in 1930, the year he married Carol Henning.

Ricketts's Influence

Steinbeck met Edward F. Ricketts at the dentist's office in the late 1930s. Ricketts was extremely bright, well-educated (but with no degrees), and, like Steinbeck, a loner and an iconoclast prone to drinking too much. Ricketts was the owner of Pacific Biological Laboratories, Inc., situated in an old house on Cannery Row in Monterey. It was an array of cluttered, messy rooms filled with whatever live or preserved specimens Ricketts could provide for high school and college biology labs and government research facilities.

Steinbeck did not make friends easily, but Ricketts was that rare combination of scientist, philosopher, nonconformist, poet, and intellectual that Steinbeck was, or at least wished he could be. So strong was their bond that traits of Ed Ricketts appear in characters in several of Steinbeck's works.

Ricketts tried to explain to Steinbeck that he need not write obscure allegories and that his characters need not represent great worldly concepts. They could merely be the fisherman, the cannery workers, the barflies, and the prostitutes, all the common citizens of Cannery Row. Ricketts wanted Steinbeck to be a "scientist of the imagination."[4] He also wanted Steinbeck to observe people he met and, like a scientist, classify them so he could use the data when necessary.

By the spring of 1931, Carol had lost her job and the Steinbecks were feeling the strains of poverty more than ever. The old Chevy was hardly in any condition to be used even if there had been money for gas. Steinbeck's only diversion was his daily walk down to Ricketts's lab and Sunday visits with his parents.

John remembered Carol's friend Beth telling them about a little valley, Corral de Tierra, where her aunt lived, and how it would make a great locale for a book about the odd people who lived there. Whether or not he used her idea has never been proved, but soon he wrote to Ted Miller to describe *The Pastures of Heaven* as a series of related short stories centered around the Munroe family who live in a small valley and interacted with an array of local folks, each of whom come to a sorry end.

On February 27, 1932, John's thirtieth birthday, he received a telegram from McIntosh and Otis that the publishers Cape and Smith had accepted his manuscript of *The Pastures of Heaven*. He was more concerned about his parents' reaction than his own. "I'm no longer a white elephant. I am justified in the eyes of their neighbors," was his comment.[5]

It was now time for Steinbeck to concentrate on a total rewrite of *To an Unknown God*, to turn it into a better constructed work. He was preparing it for Robert O. Ballou, his new editor at McIntosh and Otis, who was extremely impressed with *Pastures of Heaven*. Moreover, now he could write while breathing a bit easier. Ricketts had hired Carol as his part-time secretary/assistant for fifty dollars a month. But then, life went sour. John's young nephew, his sister Beth's son, died; John's publisher went bankrupt; John's editor joined a new publishing firm; Ricketts's wife left him; Ricketts fired Carol; and Joseph Campbell moved into the community. Steinbeck felt that life could not have gotten any worse. But it did.

Campbell was a young Columbia University–educated author who admired Steinbeck's writing and recognized his talent. Unfortunately, he also was in love with Carol. After a brief affair, he admitted everything to Steinbeck and moved to New York.[6]

The public was not impressed with *The Pastures of Heaven*. One reason may have been that it was 1933: The Depression had worsened, and unemployment rose to twelve million people. People who could hardly buy bread were clearly not buying books. Steinbeck suggested to Mavis McIntosh that she separate his book, which was really a murder mystery, into chapters and offer them to a pulp magazine for serialization.

Olive's Poor Health

The Steinbecks had no money coming in except for the monthly stipend from his father, and because of the economy there was no guarantee how long that was going to last. When his parents invited John and Carol home to Salinas for the holidays, they had to pay for the couple's trip. They also discovered that Olive was failing fast. Though she insisted on cooking, Carol needed to stand behind her to prevent her from falling over. Both the Steinbeck men were filled with dread—John Ernst because of his constant dependence on Olive and John because he was afraid his mother would die knowing him only as a failure. The pervading gloom was nearly unbearable.

In March, Olive suffered a stroke. John and Carol moved into the house in Salinas to help care for her. John spent the better part of the day at the hospital hating every minute of seeing the strong woman he remembered deteriorating so rapidly.

At that time John sporadically worked on a short story about a boy whose pony develops distemper, a fatal disease. He heard from Robert Ballou, who was determined to publish *To an Unknown God* himself. He would act as agent, editor and publisher, but his option (right to publish) on the book had run out before he had the financial backing. In the meantime, McIntire and Otis had gotten Simon and Schuster, a very prestigious publisher, to commit. However, broke or not,

Steinbeck remembered how loyal Ballou had been to him and agreed to extend his option to publish the book even though the contract had run out.

The Phalanx Theory

One day in June, as John sat by his mother's bedside, an odd thought crossed his mind. "Half of the cell units in my mother's body have rebelled . . . She, as a human unit, is deterred from functioning as she ordinarily did by a schism of a number of her cells."[7]

He remembered how this idea fit in with the ideas of biologist William Emerson Ritter. Under Ricketts's supervision, Steinbeck eventually wrote an unpublished paper called "Argument of Phalanx." In essence, Steinbeck's premise was that when you are part of a group there is no "you." You behave as the group behaves. Once a person is removed

phalanx
An organized group of people.

from the group, the person becomes a phalanx, a unit made of cells. Steinbeck based the thesis on Ritter's claim that each of the pieces of the whole is equally important to the whole's ability to function. Like all units made up of parts, Steinbeck conjectured, people in groups connect through a stronger spirit that moves them from within. Think of a school of fish all swimming in one direction. They, as a group, are the phalanx. But if one fish swims away, it is vulnerable, and the phalanx will not protect it. Therefore it must be its own phalanx. That idea would pervade Steinbeck's work from then on.

The *Paisano* Novel

Oddly, with less time to work, Steinbeck became more creative. He finished what he called the "pony book." He then went on to write the *paisano* stories based on his many encounters with the locals in Cannery Row and the stories told to him by Sue Gregory, a high school Spanish teacher of Mexican heritage who had been studying the local Mexicans living nearby in a shabby district known as Tortilla Flat. It was not a hard book for Steinbeck to write because he had had an affinity for Mexican Americans since his childhood.

By October 1933, Robert Ballou kept his promise and published *To a God Unknown*. It is a mythical tale of a man named Joseph Wayne, who tries to fulfill his dead father's dream of creating a prosperous farm in California. In the process, he finds a tree on his property that embodies his father's spirit, but one of his brothers, afraid of paganism, chops it down. Thereafter, Joseph's farm suffers famine and pestilence. *To a God Unknown* received the same kind of limited reception as *The Pastures of Heaven*. But Ballou and McIntire and Otis still believed in Steinbeck even though as a professional author of seven years, he had earned only $870. In fact, Elizabeth Otis was able to place two sections of *The Red Pony* into two consecutive issues of a prestigious monthly magazine, *North American Review*. The magazine paid Steinbeck ninety dollars. Carol found a job with the Emergency Relief Organization, a government agency that helped mostly Mexican families to find work. Her nightly tales of their horrific lives gave John more background for his *paisano* novel.

Taking long walks gave John a respite from caring for his parents. On one of his walks he noticed cars and trucks with Oklahoma license plates overflowing with furniture and people in tattered clothes. A small enclave had been set up that the Salinas people called "Little Oklahoma." Curious to learn about these displaced "Okies," Steinbeck sat down with

Steinbeck had always been sympathetic to the plight of Mexican American workers. His 1935 novel *Tortilla Flat* told the story of some of these *paisanos* using the King Arthur tales.

some of them to chat about why and how they crossed the country to find work in California. He found them fascinating and told Carol that their story would make a great novel.

On February 19, 1934, as John sat by her bedside, his mother died peacefully in her sleep.

John finished his *paisano* book, called *Tortilla Flat*, and sent it first to Mavis McIntosh and then to Robert Ballou, who both rejected it. Steinbeck then decided to follow Ricketts's suggestion that he concentrate on writing more short stories.

Communism

Because he sympathized with the downtrodden and felt an affinity for some of the idealistic principles behind Communism, Steinbeck was often accused of actually being a Communist. But Steinbeck was never a member of the Communist Party. Among the many reasons for Steinbeck's rejection of Communism was his strong belief in the individual and not in the "collective." Still, Steinbeck was interested in telling the story of Pat Chambers and Caroline Decker, two union organizers of the Cannery and Agricultural Workers' Industrial Union (C&AWIU) who were hiding out in Seaside, a small town near Monterey, to avoid being arrested for illegal strike activity. They were soon joined by Cicil McKiddy, who was instrumental in winning the cotton workers strike in Bakersfield the year before. Originally from the Dust Bowl of Oklahoma, McKiddy had been a publicist for the union in Monterey, writing and printing pamphlets about the plight of the workers, which was the reason the Monterey police were after him. Steinbeck offered to pay the three a small sum to write about them because he knew instinctively their story of labor activism was a good one.

Meanwhile, Pascal "Pat" Covici, a partner in a New York publishing company, Covici-Friede, read a copy of *The*

Pastures of Heaven and immediately called McIntosh and Otis to ask if they had any unpublished Steinbeck manuscripts. They sent him *Tortilla Flat*. Covici loved the novel and offered not only to publish it, but to republish any Steinbeck novels that had gone out of print and to publish any subsequent novels Steinbeck would write.

By the end of January 1935, Steinbeck had finished the 120,000-word manuscript of *In Dubious Battle,* but Covici-Friede rejected it. At this point Elizabeth Otis took over Steinbeck's career. She thought highly of him as an author and admired him as a person. They were actually a perfect professional pair. Otis sent the new manuscript to Bobbs-Merrill, a large publishing house, which agreed to publish it. Pat Covici was furious when he returned from vacation to discover that without authorization, Harry Black, one of his editors, had rejected *In Dubious Battle*. Black had taken it upon himself to decline the book because he thought its story of workers' rights would offend some readers. Covici fired Black and pleaded with Steinbeck to get *In Dubious Battle* back from Bobbs-Merrill and allow Covici-Friede to publish it. Steinbeck agreed, and a lifelong partnership began.

John Ernst died in May of 1935, five days before his son's new book, *Tortilla Flat*, appeared in bookstores. A retelling of the legend of King Arthur set in the slums of Monterey, an examination of the phalanx as seen in gang life, and a wry comment on possessions as economic status symbols, *Tortilla Flat* was well-received by most critics, but it was the reading public that made it a best seller. Readers enjoyed Steinbeck's comical approach and the truthful portrayal of the harsh conditions of their lives. In mid-August, Pat Covici handed Steinbeck his first royalty check. It was for three hundred dollars. John and Carol's days of abject poverty were over.

The film rights to *Tortilla Flat* eventually sold for four thousand dollars. John, accompanied by Carol, went to New York in January 1936 to sign the contracts and then returned to Pacific Grove to enjoy their newfound wealth. They soon learned that *Tortilla Flat* had just hit the best-seller list and had been awarded the 1935 prize by the Commonwealth Club of California for being the best novel about California. It earned the distinction of being one of the five best-selling books on the West Coast.

A Misunderstood Work

In Dubious Battle was published in January 1936 to generally good reviews, though not as good as those for *Tortilla Flat*. Some conservatives thought *In Dubious Battle* was a pro-Communist treatise because it depicted the exploitation of the lower classes by wealthy businessmen and landowners, while some liberals thought it completely distorted Communist ideology. The distinguished French author and future Nobel Prize recipient Andre Gide called *In Dubious Battle* "a beautiful and painful book."[8] Fresh out of Vassar, Mary McCarthy, who would become a major American author and critic, wrote a very negative review in the *Nation*. She commented that Steinbeck was "no philosopher, sociologist or strike tactician" and used terms like "childish" and "pompous" to describe his writing.[9] Steinbeck was more annoyed than pleased that his book was selling well. The critics, even those who reviewed the novel favorably, had misunderstood his message.

As part of what would be Steinbeck's Great Depression migrant-worker trilogy (*In Dubious Battle*, *Of Mice and Men*, and *The Grapes of Wrath*), *In Dubious Battle* tells of a workers' strike in the apple groves of California. Steinbeck claimed that he wrote the book to document all the incidents during the strike. He wanted to tell a story about how people on opposing sides of an issue could escalate their differences into irreconcilable conflict. It is an extraordinary exploration of mob mentality and tragic idealism centered around Jim Nolan, an everyman trying to grab hold of a shard of life. Jim, though warned of the danger of joining "the party," nevertheless is gradually pulled into the fray of the striking pickers.[10] One of the characters, Doc Burton, is based on Ed Ricketts. Doc/Ricketts continues to appear in other Steinbeck novels, namely *Cannery Row* and *Sweet Thursday*. But compared to these other novels, *In Dubious Battle* relies more on the depiction of the strike, more like a documentary than a novel.

A Novel in Dialogue

John and Carol Steinbeck had a small house built in the hills west of Los Gatos, about fifty miles north of Monterey. Carol's preoccupation with the house gave John the freedom to work on "Something that Happened," another story about farm workers struggling to retain their dignity. This was a simply told tale of how their dreams, even the smallest ones, never seem to come true; how lonely they were even when surrounded by dozens of other workers; and how the phalanx can split even the relationship of two men who never should have been so close.

As Steinbeck turned "Something that Happened" into a full-length novel, the characters began to grow and take on their own personalities through the dialogue he was writing. And it was just dialogue. There were no descriptive passages yet. More characters were introduced, and through their introduction, the plot was strengthened because each had a story to tell and each story became intertwined into the next character's story. The novel was developing exactly like a play, foreshadowing the dangers that the reader knows are there but must wait to see unfold.

Ed Ricketts suggested a new title: *Of Mice and Men,* taken from "To a Mouse" by the Scottish poet Robert Burns: "the best laid schemes o' mice an' men gang aft a-gley/ [go often astray or awry] And leave us naught but grief and pain/For promised joy." Burns's poem talks about how humans cannot control the forces of nature, a topic in which Steinbeck and Ricketts were both interested. *Of Mice and Men* was completed in mid-August 1936. It took only two months to write the thirty-thousand words, and part of that was a rewrite: Steinbeck's dog Toby had chewed up the half-done manuscript. Steinbeck sent it off to Elizabeth Otis with a note in which he said that although he had faith in this short novel, he did not think it would have mass appeal.

foreshadow

To hint at something that will happen later on in a story.

OF MICE AND MEN

Even though *Of Mice and Men* was one of the most frequently banned books in the United States through as late as the 1990s, it is, nonetheless, "simple and clear, yet profound and beautiful."[1] The narrative of the novel has roots in the legend of King Arthur—"the knightly loyalty, the pursuit of the vision, the creation of a bond and its destruction by an at least potentially adulterous relationship."[2] Written very much like a play, the novella was easy to adapt to the stage and to the screen. Because it was structured like a play, the work is full of dialogue. And when there is description, it is not of the internal states of characters, but rather of their appearance or actions, or of sights, sounds, and physical details that surround them. The descriptions are meticulous and almost like notes to a director and production designer.

George and Lennie

The first chapter establishes the relationship between the two main characters: George and Lennie. George, the embodiment of King Arthur, is remarkably pure (he has no relations with women, even when the other workers go to the whorehouses). George is very critical of Curley's wife (perhaps because he senses her danger to Lennie) and of any sexual references that are exchanged between the men, such as when Curley boasts of keeping his hands in Vaseline for his wife's sake.

A 1939 production of *Of Mice and Men*. The novel's heavy use of dialogue and Steinbeck's descriptions made it easily adaptable to the stage.

George and Lennie, two bindlestiffs (hobos), are trying to make a life for themselves in California during the Depression. George is Lennie's protector, a fatherly figure looking after his grown child. Like a father, he scolds Lennie for misbehaving, and like a son, Lennie lives to please George. George must plan every moment of Lennie's life, because he is aware that Lennie cannot do it for himself. But he knows that no matter how carefully he plans, Lennie will do something foolish, and they will have to leave wherever they are and start life anew. George is tired of caring for Lennie and regrets that he must carry this burden with him wherever he goes. Yet he realizes that with Lennie to care for, he is not lonely like all the other migrant workers who, if they are lucky, find work, finish it and move on—always alone.

Lennie, on the other hand, is too simpleminded to think about his part of their relationship. Like a child, he is only concerned with what George can do for him. He cannot understand the broader aspects of life or its complexities but can only remember small details, like raising rabbits. Ironically, Lennie is not dangerous because of his strength and size, but because of his innocence.

Lennie may be a gentle giant, but he has a capacity for great violence. For example, he complains to George during the description of the farm that he would kill any cat that hurt his rabbits. He submerges his violence because, as limited as he is, he understands that it is wrong. Thus, when Curley attacks him, he does not retaliate until George allows him to act. This incident foreshadows the terrible events at the end of the book.

Given his mental deficiencies, Lennie's need for George is obvious. George's need for Lennie is more obscure, but no less intense. Lennie gives George a sense of power.[3] George directs

39

Lennie, clearly illustrated in Lennie's fight with Curley. George is the brains, and Lennie is the brawn. Lennie is what makes George special and gives him a reason for living. At one point, George admits how much he teased Lennie when they were kids, but Lennie took all the teasing and never fought back. George recounts how one day he told Lennie to jump into the river and Lennie did it—even though he didn't know how to swim. George could never abandon Lennie's blind devotion.

Some critics have felt that Lennie was not human enough as a character. Others felt that "Lennie is not a character in the story at all, but rather a device like a golden coin in *Moby Dick* to which the other characters may react in a way that allows the reader to perceive their attitudes."[4]

Cain and Abel

Of Mice and Men offers one of the first looks at Steinbeck's preoccupation with biblical allegory. George is cast as Cain and Lennie as Abel. George volunteers to be his "brother's keeper"—he has been taking care of Lennie for years. He stays his brother's keeper to the end, when he shoots him—unlike Candy, who is too cowardly to put his dog out of its misery forcing Carlson to do it. George wants to break the curse of Cain, to stop wandering the land and actually settle down.[5] In fact, the act of murder he performs upon his "brother" is an act of "keeping" him from the mob's destructive hands. He is a "good" Cain, because the murder he performs is not motivated by ill desires. "To empathize with Cain is to reevaluate what we call evil."[6] To Steinbeck, Abel is not totally good and Cain not totally evil. Steinbeck is particularly interested in redefining Cain's role in the relationship. This theme will reappear in future Steinbeck works, such as *The Grapes of Wrath* and, most notably, *East of Eden.*

Candy

When George and Lennie arrive at the bunkhouse, they meet Candy, the swamper (janitor). He is a weak, infirm old man who owns a weak, infirm old dog. Though he might seem nosy, Candy serves as the person who introduces George and Lennie to everyone on the farm. Candy is like a combination of an old Lennie and George. He is the only man on the farm who understands the relationship between George and Lennie because he has a similar relationship with his dog. The other men do not understand because their lives are not oriented toward caring. Of necessity, they must be survivors, men who must take care of only themselves. Candy knows he is useless and he has no future. He knows he is only kept at the ranch because he was injured there and because the boss expects that he will die soon. Like his dog, he is so handicapped that he is of little use. He knows his last chance to live out whatever years he has left is to latch onto George and become part of George's dream. He offers George money, thereby giving George hope of fulfilling his dream of buying a ranch.

theme

A distinctive quality or concern in one or more works of fiction.

Curley

Curley is the son of the ranch boss. He tries to incite Lennie as soon as he meets him. Candy explains that Curley is jealous of big men and will fight them so if he loses he can claim it was their size, not their ability that caused him to lose. George explains to Candy that though Lennie is big, he does not know anything about fighting. While playing cards, Candy tells them that Curley was married a few weeks ago and since then has been wearing a glove over a hand covered in Vaseline to keep his hand soft for his wife, whom Candy accuses of being a "tart." Soon after, George, who suddenly seems frightened, warns Lennie to keep away from Curley and again reminds him where to hide if he gets into trouble.

Curley appears as the antagonist, the threat to everyone on the ranch when, in fact, he is the most insecure. Not only is he physically small, but he also knows he cannot sexually satisfy his wife and at any minute she could be with any one of the workers. He wears boots with large heels to make him appear taller and to make him feel bigger. He realizes that by fighting Lennie, he can gain some respect from his farmhands. His wife—the only female character without a name—is indeed a tramp. It is obvious that she cares about her appearance not to impress her husband but to entice the other men. And Curley knows it—why else would he be constantly searching for her? Through George's reaction when he first sees her, the reader is immediately aware that she is a threat to both Lennie and George.

Curley's Wife

Curley's wife is the lady in red: dress, shoes, lipstick, and fingernails, sensually teasing the men. George cannot deny her beauty and her allure but immediately senses what she is up to and warns Lennie to stay away from her. He knows she is more trouble than either one of them can handle. Her confrontation with the three "weak men" reveals that she knows that men dislike her. But she blames it on male insecurity. Men, she claims, are only able to attack her when they come together. Together, as a phalanx, men are strong, but as individuals, men only think of themselves. She is extremely lonely, but she realizes that the men are also lonely: Their favorite escape is

Curley's wife is portrayed as a woman who is disappointed by her life and not to be trusted. She enjoys toying with the men, as is shown here in a scene from the play.

a whorehouse in the town of Soledad, the Spanish word for "solitude."

Slim and Puppies

Slim enters the bunkhouse to tell Curley's wife that he saw Curley on his way home and to announce that the night before his dog had a litter of nine puppies, but he drowned four of them because his dog couldn't nurse all nine. Carlson, a big burly man, comes in to meet the new men and asks Slim to give one pup to Candy because his dog is old and feeble. Lennie, of course, wants a pup too, and George tells him he will try to get one for him.

Lennie's sacrifice of his own life so George could survive is mirrored in Slim's need to kill four of the pups so that the other five can live. Slim is the most intelligent of all the farm hands and understands what motivates the others.

The Women

Most of the women in the novel are viewed in a negative light. For example, when the topic of Curley's wife comes up, Whit, a farmhand, suggests they all go to a whorehouse in town that night. There are two available: one run by old Susy, the other by Clara. The fact that the whorehouse madam has the same name as Aunt Clara, who reared Lennie until her death, associates the aunt with impropriety. There is also the young girl from Weed, who accused Lennie of raping her, when all he wanted to do was touch her dress. Her accusation launches a lynch mob, from which George and Lennie barely escape.

Living Lies

All the characters in the novel are living lies. Curley knows his marriage will never work out but will not admit it. His wife knows there never was a show business career for her, but she will continue to tell the story at the drop of a hat. George knows that he will never have a farm of his own, but he keeps talking himself and Lennie into it.

Foreshadowing

Steinbeck foreshadows a number of things in this first chapter, to which he will return as the story continues: George twice warns Lennie not to talk unnecessarily. Lennie carries a dead mouse in his pocket, too ashamed to tell George that he killed it, even though it is only a mouse. George finds a safe spot in which Lennie can hide because he knows Lennie will need it.

Accidents

As George predicts, Lennie kills the puppy. Though it was an accident, it still shows that Lennie cannot control his anger. In fact, he becomes even angrier at the pup for being so fragile. Lennie is upset because he fears George's punishment, not because he feels bad for killing. Curley's wife comes upon him, and the two almost arrive at a moment of understanding. Through dual conversations—Lennie about the farm and rabbits and she about her truncated show business life—their ideas merge with a discussion of the touch of soft objects, like rabbits, velvet, and her hair. Curley's wife calls Lennie "nuts" but counters by saying he is a nice guy and a big baby. She invites Lennie to feel her hair. But when he lingers too long she claims he will "muss it."[7] Lennie can't let go and in a moment of panic, while covering her mouth to keep her from screaming, breaks her neck and kills her.

Mercy Killing

As soon as George sees the body, he knows exactly what has happened and how to deal with it. He realizes it is senseless to deny Lennie's guilt and knows that he will die a horrible death when the men get their hands on him. Candy must fight for his own life when he asks George if there is still a chance the two of them could buy a farm. At this point George finally verbalizes the truth—there never was a chance. He tells the men that Lennie must have gone south, then goes to Carlson's bunk and steals his gun.

symbol
Something that stands for, represents, or suggests another thing.

While Lennie waits for George down by the Salinas River, he is not concerned that he has killed a person. He is distraught over what George will think of him and if he will be told to go off on his own. He suffers a psychotic episode with hallucinations. He envisions his Aunt Clara as an overbearing shrew who scolds him for his wrong-doing. Then a huge rabbit appears. Throughout the novel, the rabbit has been a symbol of the gentle side of Lennie, but now it is an ogre that torments Lennie with vile threats. When George comes, Lennie urges George to recite the continuing litany about their relationship being unique and about the farm and the rabbits. George calms Lennie by telling him about the farm and then shoots him in the back of the head in much the same way Slim shot Candy's dog. As Candy should have shot his own dog, George knew it was his place to shoot Lennie. It was a mercy killing. George then tells the others that he shot Lennie in self defense using Carlson's stolen pistol.

Coming Full Circle

George undergoes a great change. Though he has constantly told Lennie that he would be happier without him, George always knew that he was incomplete without his buddy. They were like two parts of one being: Lennie, the body, and George, the brains. As much as George complained about Lennie, he actually valued and needed his friendship to feel important. Without Lennie there is no dream of a farm. When George tells Lennie about living without him, just before he pulls the trigger, the speech is delivered without emotion because George knows that this time it is a lie. George does not want to be a solitary figure—but now he must. Lennie is dead and so is the dream and so is a part of George. Slim immediately knows what really happened, but the others are bewildered about why George is so disturbed about the shooting.

There is a circular structure in the novel, evident in the neat balance between the opening and closing scenes. In the opening scene, George and Lennie climb down to the pool from the highway. And in the closing scene, George and Slim climb up from the pool to the highway. By losing Lennie, George becomes just like any other man, "destroying the thing that makes him different and reducing himself to the status of an ordinary guy."[8] However, the tragedy offers a glimmer of hope. George is not walking off a total loner—he is walking off with Slim—just two ordinary men walking off, but together. There is a bond between them—it is prescribed in the circular structure of the novel. Both Slim and George are very understanding men, and they are sensitive to what has just happened. They are not fictional dreamers, the kind George pretended to be for Lennie's sake. Perhaps their dream of owning a farm is more realizable now that they have formed a phalanx and accepted their status as average men.

THE WORLD
MUST KNOW

4

With *Of Mice and Men* behind him, Steinbeck now had time to accept an assignment to write a series of articles about migrant workers for the *San Francisco News*. He would visit various regions in rural America to observe living and working conditions. He was particularly interested in seeing how the government-run camps were helping the migrants. In order not to be too conspicuous, Steinbeck bought a bakery truck and outfitted it with bedding, cooking utensils, and all the other items he would need for his trip. He was shocked to see the cardboard boxes and abandoned water viaducts in which whole families lived. Because food was so scarce and so expensive, people were forced to eat stray dogs and cats and even rodents. At this time, such horrific sights were far from rare in the Central Valley.

By 1936, it was reported that nearly ninety thousand Okies (as migrant sharecroppers and workers from small farms who came from any of the Dust Bowl states were called) had moved to California hoping to find work or some land. These workers, mainly Bible-belt fundamentalist Christians, had left behind a homeland devastated by the Depression and drought and were now trying to find nonexistent jobs. They were accused of being ignorant, dirty, and immoral, and they were blockaded by border police, verbally battered, and physically abused. It made perfect sense that conflict between the native Californians and the migrants would occur. Locals resisted

A family of Okies travels west in an effort to escape the Dust Bowl. They carried all of their belongings on their small truck.

allowing migrants into town for fear that the children of those in the camps would overcrowd the schools, or absorb more than their share of relief funds, and that union organizing would interfere with local government. One community refused to allow "Negroes and Okies" to sit anywhere except in the theater balcony.[1]

Those who lived in squatters' camps barely managed to survive under foul conditions. Those on farms were not much better off, but they were given a piece of land on which to pitch a tent and park a vehicle. A spigot and an outhouse were made available to them. Those who were lucky enough to find harvesting jobs on larger farms lived in one-room shacks for which they were charged an unaffordable fee, ate food that had to be bought from a company store at inflated prices, and shared a shower and toilet with two hundred other Okies.

Weedpatch

In contrast to these appalling sites were the fifteen government camps, known as "sanitary camps." During August 1936, Steinbeck visited what he called "rotten and deplorable" places owned by farmers who would not use the government models. While at the Arvin Sanitary Camp, Steinbeck met Tom Collins, a sanitary camp manager at "Weedpatch," as those who lived in Arvin called it. Steinbeck was impressed with how well the camp was run. He was even more impressed with Collins, who, no matter how tired he might have been, knew what was going on at all times in every corner of his camp. As manager, he created a system in which the residents governed themselves and were permitted to make camp rules and enforce them.

THE DUST BOWL

Steinbeck's novels *The Grapes of Wrath* and *Of Mice and Men* both center around migrant workers trying to escape the Dust Bowl, which was a period of severe dust storms in the 1930s. The storms were brought about by drought and poor farming methods that caused soil erosion, which meant there were no grasses to protect the soil. That soil then turned to dust, and the winds sweeping across the plains churned up great clouds of dust so heavy that people could see no more than a few feet in front of them. With no way to grow food, thousands of farming families were forced to move in search of a better life.

Although all of the central United States were affected, the states that were hit the hardest were Kansas, Oklahoma, Texas, New Mexico, and Colorado.

When Steinbeck finally got back to Los Gatos, Steinbeck wrote to Tom Collins to tell him how impressed he was with the experience of visiting the camp and that he hoped that the articles he was about to write would help to show the plight of the downtrodden. He enclosed a sizable check to be used by the migrants for raising cattle. He also planned to send books for the children to encourage them to learn to read.

Steinbeck's first article on the migrants appeared in the *Nation* on September 12, 1936. He completed the seven articles that were commissioned for publication from October 5 through 11 by the *San Francisco News*. They were then expanded and released in a bound edition called *Starvation Under the Orange Trees* and later retitled *The Harvest Gypsies*. Some took exception to the material; others asked him to lecture about the camps. In several letters and conversations after the publication of *The Harvest Gypsies*, Steinbeck expressed his fear that the destitution and unfairness of the migrant workers' conditions might push them to violence and even lead to a civil war of sorts. He felt the situation was very dangerous.

The Little Book

Meanwhile, *Of Mice and Men* was also generating interest. The Book of the Month Club named the book its main selection, guaranteeing substantial sales. It appeared in February 1937 and within a few weeks sold 117,000 copies. Most critics thought highly of "the little book," as Steinbeck referred to it.[2]

Annie Laurie Williams, who handled film and stage contracts for McIntosh and Otis, had shown *Of Mice and Men* to Beatrice Kaufman, the East Coast representative for Samuel Goldwyn Pictures. She, in turn, passed the novel on to her husband, George S. Kaufman, the noted playwright and director, who saw immediately that Steinbeck had written this novel in play form. He brought Sam Harris on board as producer, and the two of them planned a stage production for the following fall. But the Steinbecks had already planned an extensive trip to Europe. John did some preliminary writing with Kaufman, but when April 15 arrived, the Steinbecks boarded a freighter and set sail.

In Europe, he discovered he was well-known. The Steinbecks' visit to Russia was enlightening and disheartening at the same time. John did not enjoy being considered a spokesman for the American working class. He realized it was easy to see that the treatment of the poor farmworkers in America was no different from the way Russia treated all of its citizens.[3]

When the Steinbecks returned to New York, John knew he had to get the play ready. But he was reluctant because he had never written a play before and he was eager to begin a new book about the migrant workers. Annie Laurie Williams, experienced with scripts, taught him playwriting style, and Kaufman invited him to spend a week on his farm in Pennsylvania to finish it.

John and Carol decided to drive back home to California. They bought a red Chevrolet in New York, and once they passed Chicago, they followed Route 66 through Oklahoma right back to California, the same route the Okies followed. Once home, Steinbeck set out to join Tom Collins again. When he finally met up with Collins, they spent three weeks working in the field in the Gridley area and then went on to the squatters' camp. By November 7, stockpiled with notes based on the experiences he had with Collins, they returned to Los Gatos to a huge surprise party thrown by Carol.

On Broadway

The *Of Mice and Men* opening night on Broadway was November 23, 1937. The critical response was positive ,and the audiences enjoyed it enough to keep the play running for 207 performances. The New York Drama Critics Circle voted it the Best American Play of 1938. It was cited for, among other things, "its refusal to make this study of tragic loneliness and frustration either cheap or sensational."[4]

Celebrity status began to take its toll. Steinbeck was suddenly besieged with requests for charity, handouts, and donations. Some were legitimate, like helping Ed Ricketts pay off the loans he took out to rebuild Pacific Biologicals after it burned down a few years earlier. He was even involved in a phony paternity suit to extort money from him. Worst of all, Carol seemed to begrudge John's success. She resented that after all these years she had nothing to show for herself.

Although she was responsible for turning some pretty sloppy writing into good manuscripts, she never published anything of note. Now what the couple shared most was quarrelling. Rather than attempt to reconcile the difficulties, Steinbeck hid himself away and wrote.

The Big Book

Steinbeck began writing a brand-new book, "the big book," as he called it. He had to tell the world about the plight of the migrant workers and if no one would publish his articles, he would tell his story in the way he new best: a novel that would focus on the simple, good people who were thrown into a grueling situation beyond their control. Perhaps then the public would learn what was going on. Perhaps then someone would help.

Steinbeck worked methodically each day, building slowly until the writing seemed to soar. By October, he had written two hundred thousand words. The summer was filled with interruptions such as visits from family, friends, and celebrities like Charlie Chaplin and Broderick Crawford. John and Carol had a new house built and the old house remodeled on a piece of property five miles from town. As a gift to Carol, John had a pool installed with a brass plate affixed to the diving board dedicating the pool to her. About the same time as the foundation was being poured on the new house, Carol came up with the title of the new book. They agreed it was perfect: *The Grapes of Wrath.*

By December 1938, John and Carol had finished revising the new manuscript. Carol was far more than just a typist. As she worked, she corrected grammar and syntax and rewrote awkward passages. She was Steinbeck's editor before Pat Covici received the manuscript. So grateful was John that the

The Red Pony is the story of a young boy and his life on a California ranch. It was published in several installments in magazines before it came out as a novel in 1937. This photo shows a scene from the 1949 film adaptation.

dedication to the book reads, in part: "To Carol, who willed this book."

But at that time, Covici was in trouble. His bankruptcy could easily have ended his career in publishing and could have been harmful to Steinbeck as well. Being bankrupt, Covici's assets could have been claimed by the printer. That money included Steinbeck's royalties. Immediately, John was emotionally thrown back to his early days of poverty, and he became concerned. He had a contract with Covici for five more novels. In order to break the contract he sent Covici five novels over the next five weeks that were nothing more than handwritten pages of total gibberish and demanded his advance. That quickly solved the problem. Because Steinbeck was such a valuable commodity, Covici was able to get a job at the prestigious Viking Press by guaranteeing he would bring Steinbeck with him. Viking paid Steinbeck the royalties Covici owed him and, in addition, guaranteed the September publication of *The Long Valley*, a collection of short stories. These were stories that had appeared in major magazines between 1933 and 1937. The book also included the first complete version of *The Red Pony*.

Set on a ranch in the Salinas Valley, *The Red Pony* is comprised of four different sections that share characters, settings, and themes. It is Jody's coming-of-age story, in which the pony functions as a symbol of both innocence and maturing. Steinbeck's childhood pony, Jill, was the inspiration for this work.[5]

While visiting at Los Gatos, Covici read a portion of *The Grapes of Wrath* and knew immediately that Steinbeck had written a masterpiece. He planned an enormous first printing. Steinbeck disagreed and wrote to Elizabeth Otis to restrain Covici from getting carried away over the number of books.

He thought that many people would object to his ideas and the book might not sell, putting Covici's position at Viking in jeopardy. But Covici was right. The advance sale of *The Grapes of Wrath* passed ninety thousand by the April release date— an extremely impressive number.

The next battle was over the language. Steinbeck had spent a great deal of time joining the authentic vocabulary, even if it was raw, and the speech patterns of the migrants to rhythms he created (based on actual classical music) as a style for the book. Viking, however, could not have cared less. They demanded the language be cleaned up. Elizabeth Otis came out to Los Gatos and, together with Carol, coaxed John into modifying the sometimes obscene language so the book could go forward. Steinbeck stood firm on some of the language, but relented on most. After a contentious two days, Carol tele-graphed in the changes to Viking.

Once the language issue was settled, Viking now expressed dissatisfaction with the ending. The editors thought it was anticlimactic, especially after the power of the sections before it. But Steinbeck refused to change a word, and Viking finally agreed.

There were still problems. For one, Steinbeck was a phys-ical wreck. After some tests that indicated he had neuritis and that his metabolism was extremely low, he was confined to bed for a few weeks. The bombardment of these physical ailments coupled with the strain of completing the novel began to cause him emotional problems that led to fears of real and imagined intimidation. He received threats from right-wing groups because of his defense of the migrant workers and even negative comments from leftists who did not think he portrayed the farm workers honestly and accurately. He had heard rumors that J. Edgar Hoover, head of the FBI, was investigating him, and that the Associated Farmers organization was claiming he was a Communist. He even believed that the paternity suit that had been filed against him the year before was a trumped-up charge to smear him. He began to imagine that he and Carol could possibly be in danger.[6] And the book hadn't even gone to print yet.

Things happened very quickly once *The Grapes of Wrath* was published. The first printing was almost twenty thousand copies, all issued as first editions. They were quickly sold and by May 17 there were eighty-three thousand copies in circulation. It remained a best seller for more than a year with a total of 429,000 copies sold by the end of 1939. The film rights sold for seventy-five thousand dollars, an extremely high fee at that time for a novel to be adapted into a screenplay.[7]

intercalary
Something inserted between two things or parts.

symbolism
The representation of things by use of symbols.

The Response

The first reviews of *The Grapes of Wrath* began to appear in April. As usual, some critics claimed the writing was "senti-mental" and others called it "superficial," especially in regard to the ending. Some were annoyed by the intercalary chapters breaking the flow of the narrative that, moreover, were didactic and moralizing. Others thought they made the story of the Joads more universal, showing what life was like all around them through impersonal commentary.

The prestigious *New Yorker* critic Clifton Fadiman thought "the ending is the tawdriest kind of fake symbolism," but he added, "If only a couple of million overcomfortable people can be brought to read it, John Steinbeck's *The Grapes of Wrath* may actually effect something like a revolution in their minds and hearts."[8] By and large, *The Grapes of Wrath* was a success. Charles Angoff of *The National Review* compared Steinbeck's contribution to literature to that of Melville, Hawthorne, Crane, and Norris. He believed "the book had all the earmarks of something momentous, monumental, and memorable."[9] A review in the April 17 issue of *Time* magazine claimed, "This is John Ernst Steinbeck's longest novel (619 pages) and his best novel, i.e., his toughest and tenderest, his roughest written and most mellifluous, his most realistic and, in its ending, his most melodramatic, his angriest and most idyllic. It is 'great' in the way that *Uncle Tom's Cabin* was great because it is inspired propaganda, half tract, half human interest story, emotionalizing a great theme."[10]

THE GRAPES OF WRATH

Philosophically, *Grapes of Wrath* combines:

- The American influences of Ralph Waldo Emerson's concept of the transcendental oversoul; that is, there is no sin or morality, but one big soul that we all belong to;

- Protestant pragmatism (what actually is) and self-reliance;

- Walt Whitman's love for every man and democracy; and

- Thomas Jefferson's agrarianism (equitable division of land).

And yet, though it is more about the pursuit of self-fulfillment than it is about injustice or migration, the book is still considered a protest novel.

The Grapes of Wrath essentially has three parts: the devastation, the journey, and the destination. The devastation ends at chapter ten; the journey ends at chapter eighteen; the destination completes the book. Using a correlation between the novel and the Old Testament, these three divisions parallel the Jewish oppression in Egypt, the Exodus, and the arrival in Canaan.

A further breakdown is the use of alternating intercalary chapters, or "interchapters." These sixteen short chapters take up less than one hundred pages, just one-sixth of the novel. They diverge from the narrative and express Steinbeck's ideas about migration, equality, weather, socialization, unscrupulous car salesmen, and other topics vital to understanding the migrant workers and their social conditions. Each of these impersonal interchapters links to the personal life of the Joads in the next chapter. Each is written in its own style, sometimes biblical, sometimes narrative, sometimes editorial, sometimes using a clipped rhythm, sometimes a flowing lilt— each one appropriate to the subject matter. Some subjects are trivial, but Steinbeck's technique elevates them to greater importance. A famous previous use of interchapters was by Leo Tolstoy in *War and Peace*. The variety of styles used in the interchapters prevents them from being clumped in a group, thereby splitting *The Grapes of Wrath* in two: the narrative and the non-narrative. Ironically, by refusing to blend in, each interchapter's individuality contributes to the cohesiveness of the novel as a whole.

protest novel

A novel with a message about a current social or political condition and calls for change.

transcendentalism

A movement and philosophy based on the idea that man is basically good and that human life goes beyond the experiences of the physical world.

Another technique Steinbeck uses to maintain the coherence of his epic novel is the interweaving of symbols. For example, the images of dust, the turtle, and the red ant, just to name a few, appear throughout the book.

The Personalized Group

Some critics have felt that Steinbeck's characters are not realistic. Other critics have maintained that in order to show the

A dust storm hits the town of Hugoton, Kansas, in 1936.

universal plight of humans, Steinbeck was purposefully trying to create mythic or representational characters. Many cite the preface of *The Forgotten Village* as the explanation:

> A great many documentary films have used the generalized method, that is, the showing of a condition or an event as it affects a group of people . . . [but] it means very little to know that a million Chinese are starving unless you know one Chinese who is starving . . . Our story is centered on one family . . . Then, from association with this little personalized group, the larger conclusion concerning the racial group could be drawn with something like participation.[1]

Thereby, the one family Steinbeck uses can represent more than just its personal situation. Behind that family's actions are those of thousands who are in the same predicament. That is one way of looking at why Steinbeck's characters sometimes feel unreal or larger than life.

The Drought

Steinbeck does not begin the novel with the narrative. Instead, he sets the scene on an epic scale. The first chapter is an interchapter, since none of the main characters appears, and there are no plot points. The first chapter is analogous to the first slow sweeping shots in a movie that establish the scene and paint the landscape for the viewer. Chapter one describes the drought: The dust is so thick that people have covered their faces with handkerchiefs and wear goggles to protect their eyes. The corn crop lies dead beneath a shroud of dust. No one in the Oklahoma Dust Bowl seems to know what to do.

The cadences of the lines and their phraseology are notable: They seem to be right out of the Bible. Steinbeck creates a sense of despair on a biblical scale in a manner reminiscent of the plagues on the Egyptians. This prepares the reader for a story of mythic proportions.

Tom Joad

Tom Joad is introduced in the second chapter, as he hitchhikes home from jail. He was released early for good behavior, he tells the driver of the truck who picks him up. Although the truck with its "No Riders" sign is a manifestation of corporate power, the bored driver is only human, just like Tom. Tom and the driver find common ground, agreeing on their dislike of the rich and those who pontificate. They believe only a preacher can use big words. Others who do just get them confused. Tom is presented as a likable, bright individual, although he is not educated. He later gives his views on rehabilitation: Prisons do not rehabilitate men, but there is no other way. The irony is that prison, for the poor, can be a safe haven, guaranteeing food and shelter. It is the outside world that is not so secure.

Symbols

A turtle slowly crawls across the road and is barely missed by a car. Then a truck comes by, and one of its wheels whisks the rim of the turtle shell, tipping it over and forcing it back to the roadside. With great effort, the turtle rights itself. Steinbeck sees the turtle as the farmworker who goes about his business bothering no one, but is in constant jeopardy. The turtle is also symbolic of the Joads, heading to the Southwest, ready to pick themselves up when something knocks them down. The turtle carries its half-shell of a house, much like Wink Manley, who split a house with the Joads. The truck is again a symbol of the wealthy people in big business who have no regard for the poor farmworker. The turtle foreshadows the life the Joads will lead— plodding along on their own, only to be continuously knocked over by the corporate world. Tom picks up the turtle and carries it with him for his younger brother. Jim Casy, a former minister, reminds him that one cannot keep a turtle; it must go off on its own when it needs to, much like Tom Joad.

> **Irony**
>
> The use of words to express an idea that is opposite to the words' literal meaning. (Example: When innocence is considered dangerous.)

The grapes are both a symbol of abundance and of anger. Both meanings exist in the Bible. In the novel, Grampa daydreams about the prosperity that awaits them in California: "Gonna get me a whole big bunch a grapes off a bush, or whatever an' I'm gonna squash 'em on my face an' let 'em run offen my chin."[2] Yet, grapes can also rot, especially if no one harvests them. As it states in an interchapter: "In the souls of the people the grapes of wrath are filling and growing heavy, heavy for the vintage."[3]

California represents the Garden of Eden, a symbol Steinbeck had used before. Consider Lennie and George dreaming of the farm they are going to own someday.

Jim Casy

Jim Casy is the voice for Steinbeck's religious viewpoint. His initials are those of Jesus Christ. Like Christ, he will sacrifice himself for Tom and then for others. He is part preacher, part philosopher, and part sage who is not tethered to religious dogma. At first he felt guilty by his physical attraction to the women he converted to Christianity, but in time he realized that there is no vice or virtue, there's "just stuff people do."[4] We are all part of the Holy Spirit, Jim claims, connected by one common soul. That is one of the principles of transcendentalism, an American philosophy espoused by the likes of Emerson, Henry David Thoreau, and Walt Whitman. Jim Casy feels he has lost his connection to Jesus but retained his faith in common folks as the personification of God. When the Joads invite Casy to say grace over dinner, Casy explains to the family that he cannot because he has lost his faith

---

personification

A figure of speech in which an inanimate object is treated as, or compared to, a living thing.

---

and has gone off into the wilderness just as Christ did. All he is sure of is that when people are together as one, they are holy, but when someone runs off, he breaks the holiness, though he is not sure what it really means to be holy.

Casy's behavior is Christ-like as he sacrifices himself to save Tom. Casy is arrested instead of Tom because Casy knows Tom is in violation of parole and would face severe punishment. As he is driven off, Casy smiles. He has become the martyr, giving of himself for another.

In jail, Casy learns the lesson of strength in numbers. One person complaining about spoiled beans was not enough, but when all the prisoners protested, a phalanx was created. And it rose up against the prison.

When Casy is released from jail, he begins organizing strikes. Casy has found his calling. If he could not herd his flock in the ministry, he has found a way to do it through civil disobedience. Ultimately, he is killed in the river, perhaps a reference to Christ at the River Jordan. This time he is truly a martyr. Tom avenges his death and must go into hiding before he reemerges as a disciple.

Big Business

Chapter five, the third interchapter, is written as a mock dialogue between two non-existent people. This vocal dramatization of a philosophical argument is reminiscent of the use of a chorus in a Greek tragedy. This interchapter discusses the monsters encroaching on the earth. It reveals that one tractor can do the job of a dozen farm families, so the tenant farmers on bank-financed land are told that they are no longer necessary. The bank representatives who have no interest in the farmers and no desire to be there come to evict them and it is all very impersonal. The next intruders are the tractors that Steinbeck describes as the earth's violators. Like the bank representatives, the tractors come without feeling for people or the land. If the farmers retaliate, there is no one to fight. They are not battling a person; they are not even battling a tractor; they are battling a bank. The bankers are more destructive than the dust that destroys the crops. These monsters are totally devoid of human emotions, and though the bankers purport to be there to help finance the land, Steinbeck tells us in truth they are looking for quick monetary returns at the expense of destroying the soil.

In chapter seven, another interchapter, a car salesmen tries to make a better deal by taking advantage of customers' weaknesses. He sells jalopies rather than new cars or quality used cars. Car dealers are like big business everywhere. They exploit the poor. A new car or a good used car does not reap as much of a profit as a wreck under the hood that appears to be in good condition. That is a good sale. The writing style of this interchapter changes to brisk sentences in the manner of a salesman trying to make a quick deal.

Migrant workers harvest carrots in El Centro, California. The Joad family in *The Grapes of Wrath* hope to find jobs as laborers in California after being forced to leave their home in Oklahoma.

Land

People in *The Grapes of Wrath* have strong ties to the land and, like plants, need it to survive. One example of what happens when land is taken away is seen in the character of Muley, who has become a ghost of a man since his family went west, a dehumanized being who wanders, eats wild animals, and, nearly like a primitive man, lives in a cave. The banks have made him this way. Steinbeck believes that every inroad the banks take moves people one step farther from modern civilization. The Joads, like criminals, must hide from the deputies who patrol the land that until recently was theirs. Muley compares them to animals.

Grampa does not want to leave the land and needs to be sedated and hauled into the truck. He dies before they even make it out of Oklahoma. Pa also suffers greatly when they leave the land. Land to the Joads is not merely soil, but their attachment to nature, to life itself. Steinbeck felt that owning land endows one with responsibility to the community, the latter being a necessary component for his phalanx theory.

Chapter eleven (an interchapter) shows what happens when farmlands are abandoned. Vacated houses are no longer homes. While the tractors were plowing, there was some life, but once the engines are turned off, even the tractors are dead. However, the tractor driver never had the slightest idea of what the land really was or what he was doing to it.

The weather finds an easy victim and attacks the empty houses. It is followed by a phalanx of lower animals that invade the shards of buildings, survey the vacancy, and then leave. And when there is a little rain, weeds grow up in the doorway and between the floorboards.

69

It is Steinbeck's romantic belief that the farmer, attached to the soil, is shattered by the impersonal attack on the land by the tractor and the driver who has no understanding of how much damage he has done. And yet he counters that robotic creature by personifying the tractor as a being that goes home at the end of the day, and even dies. As in many of his other novels, Steinbeck becomes distraught about people who do not understand each other or do not understand what harm they may be doing.

Route 66

Chapter twelve is an interchapter on Route 66, the famed highway of American song and tale. The route goes directly from Mississippi to Bakersfield, California. It is the road of the migrants that crosses through myriad cities, through mountain ranges, over rivers, and into forests. When it finally reaches Bakersfield, the migrants are overjoyed that they have reached their destination. But there is still need to fear. Will the jalopies make it through California, a large state? There is talk of a patrol at the California border to keep out all the workers who are coming in hordes. At its onset, this chapter seems to take on a biblical quality, almost like the story of the Israelites crossing the desert to the Promised Land.

The New America

Rose of Sharon does not share the Joads' dream of a new life. She wants to be part of the America one sees in magazines—a home, a job, a baby. She cannot put faith in the hope of finding a nice piece of land to farm. Ma Joad reasserts her hold over the family by insisting they stay together. She begins this journey with a premonition of disaster and cannot seem to lose it, but she nevertheless remains the family's center around which the others congregate. By now, however, the acceptance of the Wilsons as family, has made her domain even greater. She begins to encompass humankind as her family; she becomes the earth mother. Jim Casy plants the seed of doubt when he says that there are too many cars going in one direction. But the Joads continue.

Okies

The Okies, as they cross the country, create their own society each time they assemble at a campground. Without ever being written down, certain rules are accepted by all the migrants because they are based on common sense, common values, and common concerns. The backbone of this society is equality, so that as each family bolsters the lives of the other families, the strength of "we" is felt by all. This society does not care about wealth or superiority and therefore does not develop leaders. Its wisdom comes from its elders. Once again, Steinbeck's style takes on a biblical tone, as if the rules have been set down by God for the Israelites crossing the desert.

Anger and Hunger

Steinbeck draws a thin line between hunger and anger. Whereas only the migrants feel hunger, anger is a key motivation for both sides of the battle. Local fruit pickers are angry that the migrants came to California in such great numbers. The more men available to work, the less money farmers will have to pay. Most accept the paltry wages because they were hungry. The landowners are angry because the migrants created an underclass that embarrassed them. The migrants are angry because the owners have them over a barrel: Work for less, or do not work. A working class revolt is imminent.

Weedpatch

The government camp of Weedpatch has toilets, showers, hot water, and Saturday night dances. There are no police, and the camp residents elect a committee to make the rules and to keep harmony in the camp. Rose of Sharon not only gets to take a bath but is informed that a resident nurse will help with the delivery of her child if she is still at Weedpatch.

Weedpatch is an example of what is reasonably close to a utopian society. Residents equally share all responsibilities. Officers are elected by a fair vote. People are treated with dignity. It may not be perfect, but it is a haven for the desperately poor migrants. It is the sanitary camp that Steinbeck visited while he was working on the *San Francisco News* articles, the place he toured with Tom Collins.

The Joads begin turning back into the family they were before they left Oklahoma. The young men are working, the kids are playing, and Ma can tend to her motherly duties. Living in Weedpatch is also an educational experience. Winfield and Ruthie have never seen a flush toilet before. Some of the other residents need to be taught how to use some of the modern conveniences. But behind the dawning of this new world, trouble lurks. The banks, through the Farmers' Association, control the size of the salaries the contractors can pay. The Association will never allow the workers any say over their own lives and even concoct methods of intimidation to thwart the success of the government camps.

Although Weedpatch is the highlight of the Joads' journey and comes the closest to a working realization of Steinbeck's phalanx theory, he himself was against the government having a greater role in peoples' lives than it already did. He believed establishments like Weedpatch should be temporary, just to

A temporary migrant camp set up by Okies in California. Steinbeck was shocked by the conditions in which these workers lived, and he tried to illustrate their desperate state in *The Grapes of Wrath*.

help folks get back on their feet. "Nowhere in the novel does Steinbeck suggest that government should play a continuing role in shaping people's lives."[5]

The Family

Ma is the strongest character in the novel. She not only loses both her parents, but travels through the night next to her mother's corpse, keeping her mother's death a secret so that the family does not stop in the desert. Ma does everything in her power to keep the family together. Nonetheless, throughout the journey, the family slowly disintegrates. The dog is killed on the highway; Grampa dies of a stroke before they leave Oklahoma; Granma dies before they reach California; Noah stays to live by the river; Rose of Sharon's husband runs off; Al decides to marry; and finally Tom decides to follow in Jim Casy's footsteps. Ma must give up the family unit she is trying so hard to maintain and give herself over to the concept of the bigger phalanx—the world.[6] This already began to happen when the Joads united with the Wilsons and then the Wainwrights, and when Ma left scraps of food for the starving kids although her own children were also hungry.

When Ma leaves Tom after he tells her he must go off, she does not cry, but suddenly it begins to rain, suggesting that if we are all part of one soul, then this universal soul is doing the crying for Ma.

Tom the Disciple

Tom wants to follow in Casy's footsteps and organize strikes against the growers. Ma asks how she will know if Tom is safe or has been hurt. If Casy is right, he tells her, and we are all part of a larger soul, it will not matter if she and he are in contact because "I'll be ever'where—wherever you look. Whenever

THE GRAPES OF WRATH

they's a fight so hungry people can eat, I'll be there. Wherever they's a cop beatin' up a guy, I'll be there . . . An' when our folks eat the stuff they raise an' live in the houses they build—why I'll be there."[7] He is becoming part of the transcendental oversoul. Tom says goodbye to his mother in a womb-like cave. When he emerges, he will be symbolically reborn.

Just as Steinbeck presented Casy as Christ, he now presents Tom as Casy's disciple. Tom accepts Casy's belief that we are all part of one soul. And if it is true, then whenever people assemble to defend their rights, his spirit will always be within those men. And when people attain the dignity of leading their own lives, his spirit will be part of it. He vows that he will continue Casy's campaign for justice for the oppressed migrant workers.

The Waters

In the last interchapter Steinbeck describes the devastation caused by heavy rains. Rivers overflow and trees come tumbling down. Fields become lakes. Cars are abandoned because they no longer are able to start. The migrant tent camps become unlivable places. Finally, the worst consequences: no work, no income. Steinbeck's style reverts once again to biblical cadences.

The Joads are now living on the Hooper ranch in half of one of twelve boxcars whose wheels have been removed. The Wainwrights occupy the other half. This echoes the way they lived in Oklahoma—half-a-house per family. This also brings back the turtle, who lives in a half-shell.

Nature, at its most powerful, is responsible for the Joads being captured. They cannot leave because the river is overflowing and because Rose of Sharon has gone into labor. The water, symbol of life and motherhood, is raging out of control.

The only possible means of curbing the flooding river is through a group effort. At first, the men only think of themselves, but Mr. Wainwright's plea influences them so they now begin to think as "we" and create a phalanx to fight the river by building an embankment.

In the midst of the rain, Rose of Sharon gives birth to a stillborn child. Uncle John places the baby in an apple box and floats it in the stream, saying: "Go down an' tell 'em." Uncle John reenacts the incident in the Bible of the baby Moses being placed into the river that will carry him to safety. Alas, this Moses—who could have led the people to the Promised Land—is dead.

Steinbeck ends the novel with a sentimental moment that gently hints at a bit of hope. Rose of Sharon, whose life has been one of misery and disappointment, saves the life of a stranger by offering him her breast milk. This is another reference to the Bible: "I [Christ] am the rose of Sharon, and the lily of the valleys" (Canticles 2:1).[8] And Rose of Sharon offers up her body as Christ does his. The man suckles and a smile comes across Rose of Sharon's face, just as it did across Jim Casy's face when he sacrificed himself to be arrested instead of Tom.

The Joads have learned that they are more than just a single family but are members of a larger entity. They are what Casy had hoped all humanity would be. Steinbeck presents the idea that enlightenment is attained only once we have overcome being self-absorbed and we widen our devotion to the world at large, a family of which we are all a part.[9]

THE PULITZER PRIZE

After *The Grapes of Wrath* was published in April 1939, John Steinbeck was deluged with mail. People he hardly knew were coming out of the woodwork to ask him for a handout. They were stopping by his ranch in Monterey as if they were long-lost friends. Being a private person, he was unhappy with becoming public property. He was criticized for his Communist leanings, as they were apparent to some, in *The Grapes of Wrath*. The book was banned in several cities for its obscenity. In Kern County, California the book was publicly burned and pulled from the shelves of public schools and libraries in Bakersfield. However, it continued to be the number one best seller in America for the entire year.

Eleanor Roosevelt, the president's wife, repeatedly defended Steinbeck's portrayal of the Okies and work camps. Steinbeck was so grateful he wrote to her to thank her. He said he was being called a liar so often he was beginning to question his own personal accounts of what happened. The film releases of *The Grapes of Wrath* and *Of Mice and Men* increased public support for Steinbeck, as the films could translate for the general public the actual dimension of the suffering the characters felt. Steinbeck was awarded the Pulitzer Prize for Literature for *The Grapes of Wrath*.

One day John Steinbeck received a phone call from Hollywood. He was offered five thousand dollars a week to write movie scripts. Carol immediately got on the phone and said,

"What the hell would we do with $5,000 a week?" and hung up.[1] Steinbeck had finally achieved financial freedom.

Gwyn

Meanwhile, John and Carol were drifting apart. In June 1940, Steinbeck returned to Hollywood despite Carol's objections. He took a small apartment near his friend Max Wagner. One evening, Max took Steinbeck to a small nightclub to hear his friend Gwendolyn Conger sing. Steinbeck was very taken by her. Gwen (or Gwyn—she changed her name in 1941) was twenty, and Steinbeck was thirty-eight. But he was not yet ready to give up on his marriage to Carol.

To satisfy his yearning for science and to get some space from Carol, Steinbeck decided to go on a sea expedition with Ed Ricketts. The plan was for John to keep a log, or diary, on what he experienced. But Carol insisted on coming along. A large fishing boat was hired for the expedition, whose goal was to find out as much as possible about the marine life off the coast of California and Mexico. Steinbeck's observation of the Mexican people and how they lived compared to Americans made him realize Mexicans were happy to be Mexicans. Only Americans thought Mexicans were poor, unhappy people, because they were judging them by American standards. The expedition down to the Sea of Cortez lasted about a month, and Steinbeck's *The Log of the Sea of Cortez* was published in 1941.

Back home, Steinbeck thought about using the humor of *Tortilla Flat* to tell the stories of the people and countryside of Monterey, and he began collecting tales for *Cannery Row*. He also began writing *The Forgotten Village*, a film in which a poor Mexican family gets caught up in politics and religion. Lewis Milestone, the producer of *Of Mice and Men*, wanted

In 1940 Steinbeck traveled with Ed Ricketts to the Sea of Cortez, also known as the Gulf of California, eventually publishing his observations as *The Log of the Sea of Cortez*.

to follow up his huge success with a film of *The Red Pony*. The New York City Board of Censors rejected *The Forgotten Village*. They felt the movie was "indecent" because of the lack of clothing worn by the Mexican peasants. They also felt the film "promoted socialism." Steinbeck's good friend Eleanor Roosevelt intervened, and the ban against *The Forgotten Village* was lifted.

When they finally got back to Los Gatos, John could see his relationship with Carol had not improved. Steinbeck suspected that Carol was jealous of him and his achievements.[2] He often escaped to San Francisco to visit Gwyn. It seemed as if Steinbeck did not care if people saw him with another woman.

Carol confronted John about his affair with Gwyn in March, and by April Carol was gone. Steinbeck occupied his time by working on *The Sea of Cortez* with Ed Ricketts. He would stay at the apartment above the lab. He sent the completed manuscript to Viking at the end of July. During this period of time, Carol moved to New York. John and Gwyn moved to the Pacific Grove house and, later, to New York City. At the age of forty, Steinbeck wanted to settle down and have children.[3]

By mid-October, Steinbeck received an invitation from President Roosevelt to be part of a committee that would find ways to combat the Nazi propaganda machine. Other writers included Thornton Wilder, Stephen Vincent Benet, and Robert Sherwood, who was also a Pulitzer Prize–winning playwright. This committee was set up under the auspices of the Foreign Information Service. Steinbeck's role as a member of the committee was to meet with refugees who had escaped their occupied countries. They had stories to tell him about the resistance and how these small secret armies pledged to fend off the Germans in any way they could. This information formed the basis for his next project, *The Moon Is Down*. He wrote it as a play, much as he did when he was writing *Of Mice and Men*.

The Moon Is Down

In March, *The Moon Is Down* was ready to be published. Steinbeck was working with Oscar Serlin, a Broadway producer, to turn it into a Broadway play. When the play was produced, it ran for nine weeks on Broadway and was hugely successful overseas. The Book of the Month Club had ordered two hundred thousand copies in advance, which topped the advance order for *The Grapes of Wrath*. However, the general critical consensus was that *The Moon Is Down* was a piece of outright propaganda, with characters who had no dimension to them. A *New York Times* reviewer called it "the most memorable fiction to come out of the war," whereas other critics, such as Clifton Fadiman and James Thurber, attacked it as "fairy tale in nature."[4] It was, nonetheless, a perfect propaganda vehicle. It appeared in seventy-six editions between 1945 and 1989 and was translated into myriad languages, including Korean, Urdu, Slovak, and Burmese. *The Moon Is Down* sold more than a million copies before the year ended.

At this time, Carol Steinbeck was making strong demands for a divorce settlement. She felt she should have a portion of the material benefits Steinbeck was enjoying, since she had been very supportive of him during his early writing career. A very generous settlement was worked out. John and Gwyn moved across the Hudson River to a house in Sneden's Landing, a town popular with movie stars and other famous people who wanted their privacy. While there, Steinbeck still worked with the FIS, writing broadcasts he would send to Washington, DC, for possible airing.

Trouble With Hitchcock

In 1943 Twentieth-Century Fox released Steinbeck's film *Lifeboat,* a story about the survivors of a U-boat sinking. Alfred Hitchcock, the British director who would become famous as the master of suspense films, was asked to direct. When the movie came out, Steinbeck was furious. The script he had delivered had not been followed to the letter. Someone had changed the black character into a stock comic, a simple role. Steinbeck did not have that in mind. There were also slurs made against organized labor, something Steinbeck would never do. He laid most of the blame on the director's doorstep. Hitchcock was a man he considered "one of those incredible middle-class English snobs."[5] Steinbeck even went so far as to request that his name be removed from any mention of the film, but the studio ignored his request. Steinbeck vowed he would never again work with people he did not know and could not trust.

John and Gwyn married on March 29, 1943, and moved back to East Fifty-Eighth Street in New York. They settled into the bottom half of a townhouse, which had all the touches of home, including a fireplace and a garden, which Steinbeck especially liked.

War Correspondent

For many months, Steinbeck had expressed interest in becoming a war correspondent for the *New York Herald Tribune.* But getting approval from the War Department was difficult. Some people who were interviewed about Steinbeck and his patriotism had made negative comments. They had not forgotten *The Grapes of Wrath* and continued their condemnation of him as a Communist and a radical. He finally received clearance from the War Department and immediately shipped out, leaving his new wife behind. Steinbeck was in the European Theatre of Operations for five months. His dispatches were popular and widely read all over the world. In August, Steinbeck received permission to go to North Africa. He attached himself to a special operations unit where he was able to watch the invasion of Italy by the Allied troops. It was Steinbeck's first contact with real battle and had a lifelong effect upon him. The experience had left him with a ruptured eardrum, sporadic memory loss, and serious depression. His dispatches from the war were collected in the book *Once There Was a War*, which was published in 1958.

Cannery Row

On October 15, 1943, Steinbeck returned home to Gwyn and, to take his mind off the war, began working on *Cannery Row*, a bright, cheerful book with many unusual and funny characters. In March, Steinbeck worked with Lewis Milestone to put together a film package for *The Pearl*, a mythical story of a Mexican Indian pearl diver named Kino who finds a valuable pearl. But the greedy townsfolk try to steal it or cheat him of its value. Something that he was hoping would save his poverty-stricken family instead inspires greed, vice, and, finally, death. Concluding that the pearl is cursed, Kino throws it back into the ocean. Kino's tragedy is thereafter told as a legend in the town.

On August 2, 1944, Thom Steinbeck was born. John had finished *Cannery Row*, which would come out in January, and was in the middle of writing *The Pearl*. But he hinted to Dook Sheffield that in the back of his mind he was contemplating another "big book."

John, Gwyn, and Thom returned to Monterey and purchased the Soto House, a well-known landmark, built in 1830. John was glad to be back with Ed Ricketts, who was the basis for Doc, *Cannery Row*'s main character. *Cannery Row* is a comical story of the denizens of the poor but colorful area of Monterey that is full of sardine canneries and whorehouses.

When *Cannery Row* came out, in January 1945, it provoked many negative reviews. One critic called it a "poisoned cream-puff of American life." Another said it showed that Steinbeck had "coasted" on the tails of *The Grapes of Wrath*, calling the story of a bunch of bums and prostitutes planning a party for the retiring "Doc" of *Cannery Row* inconsequential and pompous at the same time. Nonetheless, the sales of *Cannery Row* were sensational, and the film rights were quickly sold. The citizens of Monterey, however, felt *Cannery Row* was an insult to their town and began ignoring the Steinbecks.

Meanwhile, Steinbeck went back to completing his first draft of *The Pearl*. On February 14, he left for Mexico to begin polishing it. Gwyn joined John and traveled all over Mexico, listening to traditional Mexican music, so she could write the score for the film version.

During the summer of 1945, a film company approached Steinbeck to write a script about the Mexican revolutionary Emiliano Zapata, but Steinbeck insisted the film company get permission from the Mexican government. Steinbeck had not been pleased the way *The Forgotten Village* had been completed in Mexico, and he did not want to go through that again.

Back in New York

Upon his return to New York, John bought two adjacent brownstones on East Eighty-Fifth Street in Manhattan. Gwyn

Steinbeck based *Cannery Row* on the many colorful characters he encountered in Monterey. The area, now a popular tourist destination, consisted of many sardine canning factories and whorehouses in Steinbeck's time.

became pregnant with their second child and felt thoroughly neglected as John went off to Mexico to begin filming *The Pearl*. John Steinbeck IV was born on June 12, 1946. Gwyn stayed in her bed while nannies and nurses took care of Thom and the baby. Although Steinbeck was happy about the birth of his second son, he felt that what went on at home upstairs from his basement workroom was not his business. Friends began to notice the rift between John and Gwyn. While they both liked the social whirl, John actually may have been going out more frequently to avoid confronting Gwyn and her problems. The age difference was crucial. According to some, Gwyn was acting like a demanding brat. She was still carrying a grudge against John for leaving her at very important times in her life and for supposedly ruining her singing career. The two still went out socially, and the lack of closeness between them became more obvious to their friends. Gwyn also began an affair with a man several years her junior.

Steinbeck's newest novel, *The Wayward Bus*, was published in February. The critics were not kind. In the novel, the bus travels on a little used route in California, and picks up people from all walks of life. Steinbeck was supposedly trying to use the bus as a metaphor for the United States as a "melting pot." Some critics called the book overtly sexy. Critic Frank O'Malley said *The Wayward Bus* "has no real human or universal significance. It is nothing more than an unusually dismal bus ride."[6] Steinbeck later admitted that the novel had been "a paste-up job."[7] A total of 750,000 copies were sold through a combination of the Book of the Month Club, and Viking's own printing. *The Wayward Bus* was one of Steinbeck's most successful books.

Robert Capa

Steinbeck needed something to occupy his time so he would not have to think about his unhappy life with Gwyn. He took the *Herald Tribune* up on a suggestion to report from Europe, now that the war was over. One night, he saw Robert Capa, a photographer and friend he originally met during the war. Capa suggested they go to Russia and create a journal-like book on the average Russian, about whom Americans knew very little.

Capa and Steinbeck flew to Moscow, and they immediately had trouble with their hotel reservations. It took almost a week to get permission to travel to the Ukraine and Georgia. The Cold War had begun, and suddenly everything between Americans and Russians was treated with suspicion. Every American move was closely watched by Intourist, the Russian tourist organization. Eventually, all of Steinbeck's observations would be published as *The Russian Journal*. He was criticized by some for his unsophisticated view of the Russian versus the American political agenda. But his depictions of the Russian people and the countryside were well received. Steinbeck concluded, "Russian people are like all other people in the world. Some bad ones there are, but, by far, the greater number are very good."[8]

metaphor
A figure of speech in which a comparison is made between two words or phrases that have no literal relationship.

Steinbeck was ready for something big. Upon his return to New York, he wrote to his friend and fellow writer John O'Hara, "I've been practicing for a book for thirty-five years and this is it."[9] He mentioned this idea to Gwyn, and explained that it would be fitting if they moved back to California as he proceeded with his "great work." She would not hear of it. To John, this signified the end of the marriage.

While he was in Russia both the book and the film *The Pearl* were released. Most critics thought the story was simplistic, and the book sales were not considerable. It would take a number of years before *The Pearl* would be considered a classic.

The Death of Ed Ricketts

In the spring of 1948, Steinbeck had to return to New York to have surgery on his legs for the removal of varicose veins. He recovered at the Bedford Hotel, alone. In the first week of May, Steinbeck was notified that Ed Ricketts had been in a terrible automobile accident and was not expected to live. Steinbeck immediately flew back to the West Coast. But it was too late for him to say goodbye. Steinbeck returned to the lab and burned all of Ricketts' personal correspondence to him. Steinbeck felt he had lost "the greatest man I have ever known and the best teacher."[10] For Steinbeck, physically weakened by his surgery, without a book to keep him focused, and uncertain about the future of his marriage and children, the loss of Ed Ricketts was a serious blow.

In the midst of all this, Steinbeck would set out to write his most ambitious project.

TROUBLING TIMES

Back in New York, Gwyn told John she wanted a divorce. She moved with the boys to California and, as John knew full well, was planning to demand a huge settlement. Steinbeck was alone and miserable. Director Elia Kazan came to the rescue and offered Steinbeck the opportunity to write the screenplay for *Viva Zapata!*

Steinbeck flew to Cuernavaca and dove into his work. He traveled through Mexico, doing research on Emiliano Zapata, the peasant leader of the Mexican Revolution. In September, Steinbeck returned to his Pacific Grove house. He did not write. Friends who visited him worried about his mental state.

Happily, Steinbeck learned that he would have custody of his two boys for the following summer. Another ray of sunshine was the news that he had been elected to the American Academy of Arts and Letters, along with novelist William Faulkner, poet Mark Van Doren, and the artist Leon Kroll. Steinbeck wrote feverishly through the winter and early spring to complete *Viva Zapata!*

Elaine

Upon his return to Hollywood, Steinbeck became more social and even began dating actress Ann Sothern. She introduced him to her friend Elaine Scott, who had been a stage manager in New York. Elaine was from Texas—bright, funny, and knew a lot of Hollywood and Broadway people. Elaine was in the

Elia Kazan was one of the most influential directors of the twentieth century. He and Steinbeck became close friends and worked on several films together, including *Viva Zapata!* and *East of Eden.*

process of divorcing the actor Zachary Scott. John and Elaine began dating but kept it a secret from all but Steinbeck's closest friends.

While Steinbeck was finishing his draft of *Viva Zapata!* and beginning his notes on another book, Thom and John IV came for their midsummer visit, something their father was eagerly awaiting. Elaine Scott drove up to meet them and join in the family fun. Steinbeck believed he really did have a home again. As it turned out, he was able to keep the boys well into September because of an outbreak of polio in New York.

Steinbeck thought about another idea for a play or a novel, which would eventually become *Burning Bright*, as he continued to work on the script for *Viva Zapata!* with Kazan. He also wrote an introduction to the new edition of *The Sea of Cortez*, under the title of *The Log from the Sea of Cortez*.

In the summer of 1950, Steinbeck rented a farmhouse in Rockland County, New York, and had the boys; Elaine and her daughter, Waverly; and the boys' tutor there. He was preparing for the play version of *Burning Bright*, which was scheduled to go into rehearsal at the beginning of September. The play itself was written as a morality tale, and he feared it would be "over the heads" of a regular Broadway audience. And so it was. The play opened to bad reviews all around.

The wedding of Elaine Scott and John Steinbeck took place on December 28. John bought a brownstone on East Seventy Second Street, in which they would live for the next thirteen years.

Salinas Valley, the Novel

After the honeymoon, John began writing *Salinas Valley*. He knew this was going to be another big one—"what I have been practicing to write all my life."[1] Steinbeck envisioned the book

STEINBECK'S CONTEMPORARIES: WILLIAM FAULKNER

Honored as Nobel Laureate in 1949 "for his powerful and artistically unique contribution to the modern American novel,"[2] William Faulkner was best known for *The Sound and the Fury* (1929) and *As I Lay Dying* (1930). Faulkner is considered by many one of the most important figures in American literary history.

The plot of *The Sound and the Fury* follows each of the three Compton brothers as they mourn the death of their sister Caddy. But Caddy is certainly not a saintly sister. She becomes pregnant while young, and her short and unhappy marriage become the crux of the boys' lives and of the novel.

Faulkner died in 1962.

as a family history for Thom and John IV. Although he knew it would take the form of a novel, he kept a journal where he could record his reactions while writing the novel. It is in this journal that Steinbeck dedicates the book to his children. The journal was later published as *Journal of a Novel: The* East of Eden *Letters*. It is here Steinbeck writes that he plans to tell the boys the greatest story of all, "the story of good and evil, strength and weakness, of love and hate, of beauty and ugliness," and "shall demonstrate to them how these doubles are inseparable, how neither can exist without the other, and how, out of their groupings, creativeness is born."[3]

When John's sons would come to visit, they were left in Elaine's care. The boys, who resented the absence of their father, did their utmost to act out.[4] In the early part of June, Steinbeck changed the title of his "big book" from *Salinas*

Valley to *East of Eden,* as he became more fascinated with the Cain and Abel story in the Bible. He was able to weave this story through both the Hamilton and Trask families. Steinbeck, who was always careful to do complete research on anything he wrote, found an alternative meaning for the Hebrew word *timshel,* which was very important to the end of *East of Eden.* For Steinbeck's purposes, the word no longer meant "thou shalt not"; it meant "thou mayest," and therefore gave man greater responsibility for his own actions. When Adam Trask, the father of Cal, is on his deathbed, he is asked to forgive Cal for the death of his brother Aaron. He utters the word *timshel,* freeing Cal to live without the weight of a guilty conscience and follow a new path.

Steinbeck used three hundred pencils and thirty reams of paper for this project. The original manuscript of the novel ran to 350,000 words and the journal, 75,000 words.[5] The finished manuscript was delivered to Pat Covici in a hand-carved wooden box created by Steinbeck.

A Sad Time

By February 1952, the *East of Eden* revisions were finished and Steinbeck decided he and Elaine should go abroad. While away, Steinbeck planned to write articles for *Collier's* magazine. In Spain, Steinbeck learned that his good friend, filmmaker Elia Kazan, had testified before the House Un-American Activities Committee (HUAC). Most people in Hollywood would not appear before this congressional committee because they refused to testify against their fellow artists and name names of alleged Communist sympathizers. This was one of the darkest times in American history. As the committee's power increased, it began to seem like a witch hunt. Those who were perceived to be "left-leaning" in the film industry were blacklisted, unable to work in Hollywood. Those who did testify were considered traitors to the cause of artistic freedom.

Steinbeck defended Kazan. He called him "a good and honest man," and hoped "the Communists would not cut Kazan to pieces."[6] This was a surprise to many. They had expected Steinbeck, with his extensive knowledge of the plight of the downtrodden, to sympathize with the platform of the Communist party. But his friendship with Kazan, especially after the death of Ed Ricketts, was of such importance to Steinbeck that he had to support him. On the other hand, he would heartily defend the right of Lillian Hellman, an American novelist and playwright, not to testify before the Committee. Steinbeck was a patriot, but he was also a friend and an honest American.

EAST OF EDEN

Set in the mid-1800s through World War I, *East of Eden* is the story of three generations of two families, the Trasks and the Hamiltons. Both families move from the eastern United States to California, hoping to find fertile lands and sunshine. The novel, in four books and fifty-five chapters, is based on people with whom Steinbeck was familiar. His motivation for writing this saga was to create an enduring legacy for his two sons, Thom and John IV. The characters in the Hamilton family were based upon Steinbeck's maternal grandparents. There really was a Samuel Hamilton, and the character of Olive is based on Steinbeck's mother.

Within this family saga, there are many themes. Among them are the biblical stories of Cain and Abel, Adam and Eve, and the Garden of Eden. Other themes include the nature of good and evil, saving the environment, the group versus the individual, a child's vulnerability to the actions of his parents before him, and a child's fear that his parents do not love him.

The plot alternates between the Hamiltons and the Trasks, from one chapter to another. Certain critics felt that Steinbeck set out to write the history of the Hamiltons but then got overly interested in the Trasks and would have been better off just sticking to one family. The voice of the author appears as commentary or as character, which critics and readers have found confusing, especially when the narrator uses the "I" and "we" pronouns. There is even a point where the real John Steinbeck, as a child, comes in contact with the fictional Adam Trask.

To Steinbeck, *East of Eden* was his most meaningful and heartfelt work; upon its publication adding an additional accolade as the most read American writer of the 20th century.[1]

Cain and Abel

The Cain and Abel biblical allegory, which begins through the characters Adam and Charles, is one of fraternal innocence and envy. Abel is the favored child of Adam and Eve. He is the fair-haired boy, so to speak. He is a herdsman, while Cain tends the land. Cain cannot win his father's love, no matter what he does. Cain's jealousy gets the better of him, and he kills Abel. He tries to hide this misdeed from his father, and when asked where Abel is, he implies he does not know. "Am I my brother's keeper?" he asks. Because he has killed his brother, Cain is expelled from the Garden of Eden. God protects him, however, by putting a mark on his forehead, which will prevent him from being killed. Cain is later credited with founding the first city.

Some critics have found the allegory too obvious. For example, all the main characters that typify evil in the eyes of Steinbeck have names that begin with the letter "C" (Cyrus, Charles, Cathy, Caleb). In addition, Charles and Cathy both have big scars on their foreheads. The names of all the good characters begin with the letter "A" (Alice, Adam, Aron, Abra). Yet their names are about the only thing that is obvious. The Cain and Abel parallels in *East of Eden* are not straightforward

Several of the characters in *East of Eden* are drawn from the biblical story of Cain and Abel, illustrated here, in which one brother ultimately kills the other out of jealousy.

at all; instead they weave from brother to brother, sometimes inverting themselves, making the "Abel" character evil, and making the "Cain" character good. The conclusion Steinbeck wants the reader to draw is that every person has both good and evil within and must learn to reconcile the two.

The first Cain character is Cyrus. His first Abel counterpart is Adam's mother, who commits suicide because of Cyrus's infidelity. The second "Abel" is Alice, Cain's mother. The wives are meek and good, while Cyrus is lying, cheating, and tyrannical. Being the first father in the novel, he is also an Adam-like character, the first man, father to Cain and Abel in the Bible. Yet, rather than Eve leading to his fall, it is he who brings sin and poison to his wives (in the form of a venereal disease). Since he is also the father of the novel's Adam, he could be seen as a God-like character, or, more accurately, a Satan-like character. He is even described as "something of a devil."[2]

Cyrus's sons, Adam and Charles, are the brothers Abel and Cain. In the Bible, Cain is the first-born and, therefore, his jealousy is somewhat justified because the first son traditionally received the family inheritance and the father's favor. In the case of Adam and Charles, however, Adam is born first, and so the sibling order is not disrupted when Cyrus prefers him. Unlike the biblical story, Adam actually wants to win his stepmother's affection. He resents Cyrus's attention and later confesses that he always hated him. There is no clear reason why Cyrus prefers Adam to Charles, other than his being first-born. The two details that follow the biblical story are that Cyrus prefers Adam's gift of the puppy over Charles's gift of the pocketknife and that Charles attacks Adam, although he does not actually kill him. After the attack, however, it is Charles who settles down on the farm and Adam who is exiled into the army and thereafter wanders the land.

Caleb and Aron

Adam's twin sons, Caleb and Aron, are the second pair of Cain and Abel brothers. Sam says: "Names are a great mystery. I've never known whether the name is molded by the child or the child changed to fit the name."[3] Perhaps that is why they are named after biblical characters Caleb and Aron, which are the reverse of Cain and Abel. In the Bible Caleb was the only one of his generation (together with Joshua) allowed into the land of Canaan, whereas Aron betrayed Moses by making a golden calf for the Hebrews to worship. It is as if the symbolisms of the different parts of the name are meant to balance out: the *C* in Caleb is evil, whereas the biblical meaning of Caleb is virtuous; the *A* of Aron is virtuous, but the biblical Aron is far from good.

Aron Trask has a fair complexion and is well-liked, yet physically he resembles his evil mother, Cathy. In fact, that is why Adam prefers him to his brother, Caleb. He reminds him of Cathy. Adam seems as arbitrary as Cyrus in his preference of one son over the other. If anything, Adam should dislike the son who looks like Cathy, at least after her curse on him is lifted. But even after Adam is free of Cathy, he continues to reject Caleb in favor of Aron. Although Adam realizes how a father's preference of a sibling can lead to rivalry, he repeats Cyrus's detrimental behavior.

Steinbeck illustrates the difference between Caleb and Aron using an anthill. Aron would observe the anthill, while Cal (as Caleb is called) would knock it down and kill all the ants. Cal is always seething with anger over the rejection he feels because everyone favors Aron. Aron raises rabbits, and Caleb tends to the garden, in accordance with the biblical allegory. Both strive for their father's love and also for schoolmate

Abra's love. Abra falls in love with Aron, thereby rejecting Caleb. But Caleb's cunning leads her to reject Aron's gift of a rabbit. Yet later, Abra, a wholly positive character, falls out of love with Aron because she senses a religious hypocrisy about him. For one thing, Aron becomes too close to Mr. Rolf, the self-righteous minister. He also asks Abra to be celibate with him and begins to construct a false reality around himself when he is unable to reconcile the good and evil in his nature.

Caleb earns fifteen thousand dollars by speculating on beans and presents it to his father to make up for the loss he incurred through his failed lettuce venture. Caleb is entrepreneurial, just like Cain was after his crime. His father rejects the money and tells Cal he wishes he led a life like Aron's. Caleb becomes so angry with his father's rejection that he decides to take it out on Aron. He leads Aron to the whorehouse and introduces him to their real mother. Aron is so overwhelmed by their meeting that he enlists in the army. He is later killed. So Caleb indirectly kills Aron, just like Cain killed Abel.

In a twist on the biblical allegory, Adam is persuaded to forgive Caleb his transgressions. He utters the Hebrew word *timshel*, thereby giving his son the freedom to change his fate. Caleb is then able to reconcile the good and the evil within him, which Aron could not do. Because of his abilities to face reality and also to be an entrepreneurial success, "Cal is not only the universal Everyman in the novel, but also the representative American figure."[4]

Cathy/Kate

Many critics thought the character of Cathy Ames was based, in part, on Steinbeck's second wife, Gwyn. The "Moral Monster," according to Steinbeck, is introduced in the Cathy character. She hides her evil ways under a heart-shaped face of innocence. She is a liar who knows how to manipulate the truth. She learned very early that sexuality is useful. To Steinbeck, Cathy is evil incarnate. There is no rational reason for her behavior. She is just something that happened.

In the 1950s, when *East of Eden* was published, Cathy was a sensational character. The emphasis on her blatant sexual nature was very daring. In addition, a mother not wanting her own babies was never spoken of.

The idea that Adam would fall in love with Cathy immediately and that Charles would see right through her points to Adam's assumptions about the goodness of all people and Charles's more realistic assessment of himself and others. He still sees himself as the child who was never loved by his father. The idea that we may not be in charge of our own fate and may be subject to the randomness of nature and events was a philosophy constantly on Steinbeck's mind. He desperately wanted his own sons to find their own way and be successful in life despite having a troubled mother and a father who found it difficult to express his deep love for his children.

One of the reasons Cathy (or Kate, as she is known at the whorehouse) commits suicide is because she no longer has a terrifying effect on people like Adam and Caleb. Caleb tells her his wickedness is his own, not hers. Cal is clearly different from his mother because he has a conscience; he is constantly conflicted over hurting Aron. He loves Adam and Aron. Cathy, on the other hand, never loved anyone and only rejoiced in her evil deeds.

When she dies, Cathy leaves all her money to Aron, possibly in one last attempt to destroy him.[5] Gifts of money do not lead to good things in *East of Eden*. Caleb's fifteen thousand dollars led to rejection, anger, murder, and guilt. In fact, he had to burn the money. A generation prior to that,

Steinbeck stands with his son Thomas. He wrote *East of Eden* in the hopes that it would serve as a legacy for both of his sons, with whom he had a somewhat strained relationship.

Cyrus left his sons a fortune that he had accrued by cheating. Perhaps the theme of wealth as corruption is indicative of Steinbeck's fear that money would be the only thing his sons would take away from him.

The Voice of Reason

Lee is Adam Trask's Cantonese cook. Many critics felt he is far too convenient and wise to be a real human being.[6] Lee, like Sam Hamilton, is there to help Adam and his sons with good advice. Some critics believe the character of Lee was based upon Joe Higashi, the Japanese houseboy whom the Steinbecks hired at their Los Gatos ranch.

In chapter fifteen, Sam and Lee have a philosophical conversation in which Steinbeck speaks his message on racism in America through both characters. Sam asks Lee why he speaks "pidgin," when he is able to speak perfect English. Lee tells Sam that is what people expect from a Chinese man. Lee and Sam talk about stereotyping. Sam asks why Lee still wears a long braid (or queue) if he is no longer a slave to the Mandarin Chinese. Lee explains it would not make a difference. People still will see him as Chinese no matter what he did. In Lee's case, his physical appearance prevents him from "fitting in." Lee also tells Sam that he tried going to China, but the Chinese people considered him a foreigner as well. Lee tells Sam he is a servant because ". . . a good servant is the refuge of the philosopher . . . a good servant can completely control his master."[7]

Ironically enough, Lee discloses the true meaning of the Hebrew word *timshel* to Adam. Lee had to go to Chinese philosophers to learn this meaning. Therefore, Lee is the truest proponent of free will in the novel. He firmly believes that children do not have to repeat their parents' mistakes. Lee also retells the story of Cain and Abel with an added emphasis on the role rejection plays in the course of events. He suggests that rejection led to anger, murder, and guilt. Lee concludes that this is the story of every man, since he believes all of mankind originated with Cain. Lee notes that all men repeat the mistake of rejecting their children, which leads to anger and worse.

Lee is the voice of reason throughout the novel. He helps save Caleb from ruin. Lee discloses to Cal that his mother committed suicide. He talks about two opposites in human beings (weak/strong and cruel/kind). Lee tries to convince Cal he is not all evil, even if he did make Aron run away. Abra argues the same point with Cal. She is like an extension of Lee, who even says he wishes she were his daughter. Abra maintains that the reason Aron ran away is because he could not deal with the truth about his mother. According to Abra, Aron created a story of a world he wanted to live in and the truth about Cathy did not fit into his story. Aron was unable to deal with reality. Abra tells Cal that the reason she likes him is that he does not live in a story.

Lee tells Adam it was because of his rejection that Cal inadvertantly caused the death of Aron. Lee persuades Adam to help his only living son by giving him a chance to live without this rejection. He asks Adam to bless him. Adam says "*timshel*," thereby granting Cal the free will to overcome his guilt and go on with his life.

Good and Evil

According to Steinbeck, all art concerns itself with just one story: "All novels, all poetry, are built on the never-ending contest in ourselves of good and evil."[8] At the beginning of *East of Eden*, Steinbeck discusses what he thinks is the meaning of life and of death. He believes all men will ask at the end of their lives if they have done good or evil. To illustrate his point, he tells the myth of Croesus, the richest man in the world. Croesus asks why he is not on the list of the luckiest men in the world. Solon, the wisest man in the world, replies it is because he is not yet dead, implying those who are dead are the luckiest because they no longer struggle with good and evil.

Steinbeck says the measure of a man is whether he was loved or hated after he has died. The best man is the man who tries to elevate men to dignity, bravery, and goodness when times are bad. When he dies, people are lost without him. Sam Hamilton is an example of such a man, because his son is lost without him.

A perfect illustration of the struggle between good and evil is the coexistence of churches and whorehouses. Steinbeck claims they are two sides of the same coin. A church could lift a man out of his sorrow and so could a whorehouse. The church was the center of the Salinas Valley's cultural life, from birth to death. The whorehouses were always there as well. Throughout history, brothels were accepted as a necessary evil.

Steinbeck concludes that people have individual responsibility to struggle with the forces of good and evil and to make of life what they will.

Fathers: Wise, Loving, and Bad

Although Adam realizes that Cyrus was a bad father, he repeats Cyrus's mistakes. After Cathy shoots him and leaves, he falls into such a deep depression that he does not even notice his boys. In fact, he does not even bother to name them. It is Sam who shakes him out of his stupor. Sam physically and verbally assaults Adam and makes him name the twins. He also encourages Adam to resume planting his garden. When Adam protests, Sam tells him though things have changed for Adam, the garden will always be within him, and he has the power to create it on his ranch. Furthermore, Sam shocks Adam when he tells him of Cathy's new life. The death of Sam Hamilton is the catalyst that makes Adam change. He visits Cathy/Kate and realizes she no longer has an emotional hold on him. He is now free to live his life and to be a father to his boys. Even so, Adam favors Aron over Cal.

Sam Hamilton is portrayed as a wise and loving father, yet he fails to prepare his children for life without him. He was the life of the family, but after his death, the family crumbles. Tom is unable to outlive the guilt he has about causing Dessie's death and invariably commits suicide.

After Sam's death, Lee takes Sam's place in Adam's life. He continues giving him timely advice, including persuading him to forgive Cal at his deathbed. Although Lee is childless, he does the best job of being a father. He takes care of the twins when Adam is too depressed to notice them. As they grow, he gives them his full respect, without expecting adult reactions from them. He is always there to listen to them and offer counsel. He is the one who makes Cal realize he is not bad and that he has the will to change his life.

Steinbeck himself did not learn Adam's lesson. He always had a hard time showing love to his boys. He thought that writing this book would prove his love and alleviate brotherly rivalry between the boys. However, consider how Thom and John must have felt when they were old enough to understand the book. They were not sure which of them was supposed to be Cain and which Abel. It is true that Steinbeck wrote in his journals that he was concerned about Thom's well-being, meaning he thought Thom to be the Abel-like character.

But the boys caused so much trouble growing up, they both seemed like Cains at times. Regardless, it is a rather strange legacy to leave to one's two sons: a novel in which only one son succeeds.

Myth and Morals

Many critics felt that Steinbeck had lost his ability to write believable characters. Most agreed that the characters of Cathy, Lee, and Sam are not really human. Yet some critics took this as a symbolic level to the novel: "[B]esides being individuals first, and types second, the characters are also something else: they are symbols."[9] In fact, in his diaries, Steinbeck wrote that he was trying to "emphasize symbolic meaning over narrative description."[10] It seems as if Steinbeck placed *East of Eden* in a style between realism and allegory. The novel has very realistic concerns, such as Caleb's moral dilemma, but it also looms on a biblical or mythical level, with philosophical passages and characters that represent only one quality at a time. Cathy is a one-sided representation of evil. Sam Hamilton spouts goodness, wisdom, and reason. "Samuel's speech, attacked for being unrealistic, is elevated to the level of music to counter-balance the realistic narrative of the Trasks."[11] The character of Lee is more complicated than the first two. He is a benevolent sage like Sam, but he disguises himself as an immigrant. Unlike Sam, he does not seem to have a life of his own—he is planted at Adam's side, seemingly in order to help the Trask's survive. Lee is a mediator between the Trasks and their fate. His "specific role in the first half of *East of Eden* is the translator of the mythic into human terms."[12]

The first half of the novel is significantly more mythical than the second, with Cathy, the "Moral Monster," on the prowl and Sam, the wise wizard. The second half is more down-to-earth; Sam is no longer present, and Cathy's influence diminishes until it is gone. The second half takes a turn into more identifiable territory, as it focuses on Caleb's internal struggle.

Phalanx and the Individual

Steinbeck makes reference to the phalanx theory when he writes about the experience Adam has in the army. The army makes Adam much stronger and teaches him to no longer fear Charles. As the novel continues, however, Steinbeck puts the phalanx theory to rest. He argues that it is the individual who is important, and not the group. Although the group makes people stronger, they must not lose their individuality. "Nothing was ever created by two men. There are no good collaborations whether in music, in art, in poetry, in mathematics, in philosophy . . . the group never invents anything."[13]

The ideal group in this novel is the family. Those who lack family are not leading the right kind of life (like Cathy and Charles). At the end of the novel, Caleb and Abra are about to start a family.

TRAVELS AND POLITICS

The Steinbecks arrived in Rome and received word that Elia Kazan, who had finished reading *East of Eden* in galley form, wanted to make a movie of it. *Viva Zapata!* had recently been released in the United States and was enjoying great box-office success. Advance orders for *East of Eden* had reached more than one hundred thousand copies. However, the Book of the Month Club did not release the book under its banner as it usually did, because of the controversial character of Cathy Trask.

Elia Kazan originally wanted Marlon Brando for the role of Cal in his film version of *East of Eden*, but then he stumbled upon James Dean. When Steinbeck saw Dean, he told Kazan that Dean was a "snotty kid," but said he was right for the part, "sure as hell."[1] Kazan identified with the unlikable Caleb Trask who comes out on top, because he himself was being treated as an outcast for naming names to the HUAC in 1952. The film poster's tagline was: "Sometimes you can't tell who's good and who's bad!"—a message that both Kazan and Steinbeck could apply to their lives.[2]

While *East of Eden* jumped to the top of the best-seller list, the reviews, as usual, did not follow suit. The *New York Times* daily review by Oliver Prescott was truly a back-handed compliment: ". . . clumsy in structure and defaced by excessive melodramatics and much cheap sensationalism though it is, *East of Eden* is a serious, and, on the whole, a successful effort

James Dean became an instant movie star after appearing in the 1953 film adaptation of *East of Eden*. Steinbeck did not care for the actor personally but agreed that he was right for the part.

to grapple with a major theme."[3] And Leo Gurko in the *Nation* wrote, "This is the longest and most ambitious of the six novels by Steinbeck since the appearance of his masterpiece, *The Grapes of Wrath* . . . and raises the question of why Steinbeck's talent has declined so rapidly and so far."[4]

Pipe Dream

In 1953 John began work on a short play/novel, which he tentatively titled *Bear Flag*. Steinbeck was still trying to make a musical of *Cannery Row*, in addition to writing notes about all the people in Monterey. During the summer, Elaine took care of the boys and her daughter, Waverly. It was no easy task, complicated by John's frequent absence. She felt the boys resented her because of Gwyn's negative influence. In his autobiographical book, *The Other Side of Eden*, John IV makes the point that there was nowhere he could call home because he was driven crazy by his mother and had Elaine to contend with, whereas all he really wanted was the company of his father.

In September, John rented a house in Sag Harbor, on Long Island, New York. He liked being there because it reminded him of Monterey, and the people were ordinary and not put off by his celebrity. But when he returned to New York City, Steinbeck came down with a mysterious illness that caused him to spend ten days in the hospital. Elaine thought the illness was psychological in origin. But, in fact, it was discovered later Steinbeck had suffered a series of mini-strokes. Even though Steinbeck received the best of care from the finest New York doctors, there were no high-tech imaging machines at the time that might have found the problem. And there was no medication that might have prevented further strokes.

When the Steinbecks returned home, Oscar Hammerstein II called him and told him he had a deal. The title of the play had changed from *Bear Flag* to *At the Bear Flag Café* to *Sweet Thursday* and, finally, to *Pipe Dream*.

With very little to keep him in New York, Steinbeck decided that he and Elaine should go to Europe. He thought he would keep a travel journal, and sell his observations to various travel and lifestyle magazines. John and Elaine headed first to Spain. While there, Steinbeck suffered from another series of strokes. He was informed in Spain that his heart was abnormally small to do the work for such a large body. After some rest, John and Elaine drove to Paris. They stayed in a very elegant apartment, where his neighbor was the president of France. While there, John received word that Richard Capa had been killed by a land mine in Vietnam. It immediately threw Steinbeck into another depression. With Ricketts and Capa gone and his health failing, Steinbeck began to contemplate his own mortality.

His gloom was brightened by the arrival of his boys. As Steinbeck proudly remarked, "They are like small men with incredible bodies and quick wits."[5] He also wrote to his psychiatrist as therapy for his depression. Moreover, the continuing adulation of the French public was a good antidote to his sadness.

The Steinbecks spent Christmas in New York, with all the parties and trimmings, and, in January, they welcomed the Southern writer William Faulkner to their home. Unfortunately, Faulkner was drunk and sullen most of the time, and it was not a pleasant experience for anyone. A few months later, Faulkner, this time sober, offered his apologies to the Steinbecks.

Steinbeck bought a home in Sag Harbor in February. He proceeded at once to redesign and repair it. He also bought a new boat. He worked on the house through the spring. It was good therapy for him.

In April, through his relationship with Elizabeth Otis, Steinbeck met with Norman Cousins, the distinguished publisher of the *Saturday Review*, a weekly, general-interest magazine. Steinbeck developed a very close relationship with Cousins, and he became an editor-at-large at the magazine. He contributed many articles, on such topics as the role of the United Nations and on juvenile delinquency. Steinbeck was a good essayist and journalist, and his work was well-received. After a relaxing summer in their house in Sag Harbor, John and Elaine returned to New York in anticipation of the Broadway opening of *Pipe Dream*, even though the critics had panned its Boston opening. Steinbeck felt the characters were not "earthy" enough. "You've turned my prostitute into a visiting nurse," he wrote to Hammerstein.[6] *Pipe Dream* opened on Broadway at the end of November to lukewarm reviews. Had it not had an advance sale of one million dollars, the show would have closed before it reached 246 performances. For Steinbeck, it was the end of his playwriting experience.

Pippin

John decided to write a satirical novel about an individual who would become king, indicating intellectuals did not make good politicians. This became *The Short Reign of Pippin IV*. After the Christmas holidays, the Steinbecks, as was their regular habit, went south. They rented a yacht and cruised the Windward and Leeward islands in the Caribbean in January. In February, the couple returned to Sag Harbor. Steinbeck wanted to concentrate on his Pippin novel and needed solitude.

John also wrote a short story, which appeared in the March issue of *The Atlantic Monthly*. It was called "How Mr. Hogan Robbed A Bank" and would reemerge as *The Winter of Our Discontent*, Steinbeck's last novel. Set in a fictitious New England town, the story revolves around the moral downfall of Ethan Hawley, a descendant of Pilgrims, Harvard grad, and one-time successful business owner who is down on his luck, as he succumbs to his family's insistent cries for a comfortable life. Ethan's tale is meant to symbolize the general degeneration of American morals after World War II due to materialism or conspicuous consumption.

That summer, John and Elaine were once again hosts to John IV and Thom in Sag Harbor where Elaine's daughter, Waverly, was to be married. Elaine was very busy taking care of arrangements, and this time John had to take care of the boys, who were growing more delinquent as they got older.

Political Involvement

On August 10, 1956, the Steinbecks flew to Chicago, where John was to cover the Democratic Presidential Convention. At a small political dinner, they met Adlai Stevenson, the front-runner for the nomination. Steinbeck was very impressed with the man. He also became fascinated with the political rituals of the party and the campaign. Throughout his coverage of the convention, John wrote little anecdotes about the people he observed. He enjoyed the people he was meeting and the writing but was becoming exhausted. At the end, he hoped he would never have to cover another convention. Steinbeck ended up writing many speeches for Stevenson and his staff, but Stevenson lost the election.

During the winter, Steinbeck began work on a modern English version of Malory's *Knights of the Round Table*. He

When they were not traveling abroad, Steinbeck and his wife
Elaine divided their time between New York City and Sag Harbor.

found original documents at the Morgan Library and enjoyed uncovering new material. Steinbeck believed Malory might have gone to Italy as a soldier of fortune. Steinbeck decided he had to go to Italy to find some proof that his suspicion was correct. With Elaine and his favorite sister, Mary, Steinbeck sailed on March 25, 1957, to Naples.

Meanwhile, *The Short Reign of Pippin IV* was published. Steinbeck wanted Pippin to be a great epic like *The Grapes of Wrath*. But he was far removed from that era, just as he was far removed from Monterey. The book sold well, in spite of poor reviews. In the end, it remains the least popular of Steinbeck's novels. *The Short Reign of Pippin IV* imagines what would happen if the monarchy were restored to France. Basically, Steinbeck wanted to compare Americans and the French. The negative aspects of American materialism emerged as a new theme in Steinbeck's work and would run through *The Winter of Our Discontent* and *Travels with Charley*.

HUAC, Again

In May, the Steinbecks went to Florence. John was distressed to learn that Arthur Miller, the distinguished playwright, had been indicted by the House Committee on Un-American Activities for refusing to testify. Steinbeck wrote an essay published in the June 1957 *Esquire* magazine in which he condemns the HUAC and defends Arthur Miller. In the essay, he compares the HUAC to Russia, where "we have been revolted by the Soviet Union's encouragement of spying and telling, children reporting their parents, and wives informing on their husbands. In Hitler's Germany, it was considered patriotic to report your friends and relations to the proper authorities. And we in America have felt safe from and superior to these things. But are we so safe and superior?"[7] He wrote to Pat Covici that too many artists were cowards for not standing up for "Artie" and that he felt "a lonely sorrow and shame" for waiting so long to defend him.[8]

Abandoned Projects

Steinbeck could never avoid the voice of literary critics. This time, it was a review by Alfred Kazin of a book about Steinbeck. Kazin had nothing good to say about Steinbeck and called his later writings "cute and sentimental."[9] What was worse was that this review appeared on the front page of the prestigious *New York Times Book Review* and thus received wide attention. It bothered Steinbeck, so late in his career, to be treated this way. He knew he had to write something to convince himself, if not the critics. He decided he had to get away from America and all its external pressure.

At the end of February 1958, the Steinbecks closed down their home in Sag Harbor and sailed to England. The filmmaker Robert Bolt had rented a home for them in Somerset, and John and Elaine were very happy. Elaine was overjoyed with her husband's response to his new environment. On the last day of April, the Steinbecks visited "Camelot," the place where King Arthur supposedly held court. This dream-like existence could not last for long. John IV was having trouble in school, and Waverly was in the process of a divorce. These pieces of news made Steinbeck immerse himself further into his writing, but no matter what he did, the writing was not going smoothly. He sent a few chapters to Pat Covici and Elizabeth Otis, but their responses were not encouraging. By mid-October, Steinbeck realized his quest for Arthur and his vision for writing a new translation of Malory were coming to nothing. He decided to close up the Somerset home.

A Downward Turn

When they returned to New York, Elaine noticed certain changes in John that troubled her. One day, she smelled something burning. She ran up to his room. He was unconscious, and the cigarette he was smoking had fallen out of his fingers and ignited the mattress and his pajamas. Elaine quickly put out the fire and called an ambulance. John had suffered another small stroke, and the attack signaled the final downward turn in Steinbeck's health.

The Malory experience had depressed Steinbeck, and his recovery was slow. For weeks afterward, even until Christmas, his speech was uncertain and he temporarily lost the agility in his fingers. He wrote to Elizabeth Otis that he was going to rest for a while. But that was next to impossible for Steinbeck. During that period he said to Elia Kazan: "I have nothing to write about anymore . . . The job of a writer is to tell about his time. I've been too concerned with what's past . . . I've also lost touch with the country. I don't know what's happening out there anymore."[10]

Soon after the New Year, Steinbeck began work on *The Winter of Our Discontent*. This novel emerged as a result of his failure to write the Malory book and his disappointment with the moral decay and materialism of Americans. He also continued to write articles for *Saturday Review*, *Esquire*, and *Holiday*. In March, he wrote to the *Courier-Journal* that he wanted to do a series of articles under the byline of "The Old Curmudgeon."

Steinbeck also received letters from well-known universities asking if he would like them to bestow an honorary degree upon him. Steinbeck became very angry. He never got a degree from Stanford. Why should he accept a fake degree at ceremonies where he did not wish to be and did not wish to speak?

Another American Journey

Steinbeck wrote through the spring and expected he would finish *The Winter of Our Discontent* during the summer of 1959. He decided that as soon as he finished the novel, he would take off and learn about his country. He would travel by pickup truck, with a room inside the truck. He wanted to go alone and just listen to the sounds of America and the voice of Americans. He did not want anyone to recognize him; he just wanted to record what America was all about. He felt he did not know it anymore. Elaine was frightened. She felt Steinbeck was not healthy enough for this trip.

Meanwhile, Steinbeck was still working on *The Winter of Our Discontent*, which was to be set in Sag Harbor. But he kept very quiet about it. As "The Old Curmudgeon," he sent a letter to Adlai Stevenson in which he said that Americans' lack of morality was in direct relation to having or wanting too many things. "If I wanted to destroy a nation, I would give it too much, and have it on its knees; miserable, greedy, and sick."[11] The letter was leaked to the press, causing a minor furor. People argued on both sides. The revered poet Carl Sandburg said, "Anything John Steinbeck says about this country should be listened to. His record of love for his country and service for it is such that what he says is important."[12]

John completed a draft of *The Winter of Our Discontent* and sent it to Elizabeth Otis in July. Stevenson suggested that Steinbeck make a cross-country trip, much as he himself had been doing during his campaigns, to rediscover America. And so John hopped in a truck with Elaine's poodle, Charley, on September 23, 1959. He was going to check on the pulse of

In 1959 Steinbeck and his poodle, Charley, traveled around the country in an effort to get to know the "real" America. The result was the travelogue *Travels With Charley: In Search of America.*

Americans and, of course, he wanted to prove to himself and everyone else that he could still take care of himself.

The book, *Travels with Charley*, opens with Steinbeck's experience with Hurricane Donna, one of the worst hurricanes to hit the East Coast. He describes how the storm was pushing his boat, the *Fayre Elayne*, out to sea. This was one possession Steinbeck did not want to lose. So he jumped into the water, swam to the boat, got in, started it, and anchored it in the bay. It was quite a feat for Steinbeck, considering his physical weakness.

In his travels he reveals his sense of ecology, long before there were environmentalists. He commented that at every town he visited, a town dump loaded with car wrecks and debris of all kinds always greeted him. He thought Americans had lost their souls, especially in trailer parks, where he noted the lowest rung of people lived. He thought trailer park people were alien and could not typify mainstream America. He traveled up and down Route 90 to Chicago and then headed west.

John met Elaine in Seattle and they drove south to California. After a visit with Elaine's family, John drove to New Orleans to witness for himself how the schools there were being integrated. He stood on the sidelines and watched young white mothers spit and jeer at the tiny black children who were going to school. No one recognized him. He told them he was from England, and bystanders told him the whole integration business was the fault of the Jews. He returned to Sag Harbor. He had completed his trip in eleven weeks.

Steinbeck immediately set to work writing *Travels with Charley*, based on the copious notes he had taken during the trip. He felt quite good that this mission was completed with very little harm done to his health.

Steinbeck attended the 1961 inauguration of President John F. Kennedy with his friend John Galbraith. He wrote to President Kennedy to let him know how impressed he was with his speech, and he received a follow-up note from the president, with apologies for not having had the chance to meet him personally.

The End of Fiction

Steinbeck and Elaine returned to Sag Harbor in mid-April 1961, where he continued working on *Travels with Charley*. He did write to Pat Covici that he thought the writing was "formless." Nonetheless, *Holiday* magazine published excerpts from *Travels with Charley* to much acclaim. In June *The Winter of Our Discontent* was published. It was a story of a basically good man who becomes distressed at the way America and Americans were turning out to be greedy and amoral. Most of the reviews were lukewarm, although one reviewer for *The Atlantic* wrote that "not since *The Grapes of Wrath* had he managed such natural and realistic conversation."[13] Ironically, Steinbeck was depressed because he realized all the critics, good and bad, always came back to *The Grapes of Wrath*, as if he could never grow any further as a writer. *The Winter of Our Discontent* was the last novel Steinbeck would write. He was finished with fiction.

An Extended Trip

As more of his peers and friends died, Steinbeck thought more and more about his relationship with John IV and Thom. He decided he wanted to give them a gift that would be a legacy for them and their heirs. It would be an extended sailing trip. His plan was to take Thom, John IV, Elaine, and a tutor and travel around the world slowly for an entire year. This was an ambitious undertaking. The tutor was Terrence McNally, who later would become a well-known, award-winning playwright. Steinbeck drew up an extensive but flexible itinerary from England to Italy, to Egypt, to Japan, to Australia, and parts in-between, and finally back to San Francisco.

They sailed to England first; McNally was amazed at how much Steinbeck knew. But Elaine was noticing friction between Thom and Terrence. It seemed both Thom and John IV thought of this trip as a vacation, which they did not want spoiled by any schoolwork. This caused major arguments between Steinbeck and the boys. After England, they went on to France and then Italy. On November 25, in a hotel in Italy, Thom got into a fight that angered Steinbeck. Then, in a split second, Steinbeck fell unconscious. The boys stopped fighting and ran for help. The doctor could not tell if it was a heart attack or a stroke.

Once again, Steinbeck recovered. While John and Elaine headed for Rome where John was to have a special audience with Pope John Paul XXIII on Christmas Eve, Terrence took the boys around Northern Italy. They all met in Rome for Christmas.

In spite of a very pleasant reunion with the boys, Steinbeck's health was still precarious, made worse by the news of the death of Harold Guinzburg, his publisher. Elaine and John decided he could not endure an entire world tour. The boys and Terrence went around the Mediterranean, while Elaine and John stayed on the Isle of Capri. Between April and May, John and Elaine joined the rest of the Steinbeck contingent in Positano, Italy, and finally returned to New York in late May, after touring the Greek Islands.

The Nobel Prize

The publication of *Travels with Charley* coincided with Elaine and John's return to Sag Harbor. This time, there were some good reviews. The *New York Times* said it was "a pure delight." *Newsweek* called it "highly entertaining."[1] And the *Atlantic Monthly* said, "This is a book which should be read slowly for its savor; and one which, like Thoreau, will be quoted and measured by our own experience."[2] *Travels with Charley* moved to the top of the best-seller list almost immediately.

One night in late October 1962, John was watching television when he suddenly learned that he had won the Nobel Prize in Literature. He and Elaine began dancing around as the phones rang off the hook. The next day, there were some seventy-five reporters and cameramen waiting to meet with Steinbeck. They asked many questions, to which Steinbeck replied as best as he could. He said, "This prize is a monster,"[3] which is a reference to the many writers who received the Nobel Prize and never write again.

For Steinbeck, the reaction by his critics to his winning was difficult to handle.

The *New York Times* wrote that, while it did not want to detract from the honor Steinbeck had received, "Perhaps a poet or critic or historian—whose significance, influence, and sheer body of work had already made a more profound impression on the literature of our age" should have won.[4]

While John was trying to calm his family and his friends, telling them the comment was not important, it certainly was. His constant battle with the critics had reached its lowest point. John wondered why the awards of previous Nobel Prize winners were never questioned. Steinbeck felt unfairly singled out. He tried to put that aside in favor of the many congratulatory messages from around the world.

John, Elaine, and Alice Guinzburg, the widow of Harold Guinzburg, flew to Sweden on December 8. No sooner did they deplane, than they were feted at many dinners and luncheons given by the Swedish government, Steinbeck's Swedish publisher, and the United States Embassy, to name a few.

Steinbeck's Nobel speech was short but powerful. It was not likely he would have a platform as prestigious as this one again, and he chose his words very carefully. While he was honored to receive the award, Steinbeck said he did not want to speak as a "grateful and apologetic mouse, but to roar like a lion out of my pride in my profession." He referred to his critics as "an emasculated critical priesthood singing their litanies in empty churches."[5] Then he mapped out the role of the writer in the age of the Cold War. He encouraged writers to write about man's worthy aspirations but warned them not to ignore the power of man who had reached God-like proportions. Man now had the power to destroy the entire earth. It was the responsibility of the writers to point this out in all its ramifications through their literature. He acknowledged the irony that the giver of the prize, Alfred Nobel, was himself responsible for the production of explosives in the United States.

The Steinbecks came home a few days before Christmas. But even that holiday could not be enjoyed completely. Arthur Mizener, another critic who did not think Steinbeck should receive the Nobel Prize, weighed in. In his essay, he says after

Steinbeck stands with fellow Nobel Prize recipients in 1962. They are, left to right: Maurice Williams, Max Perutz, Francis Crick, Steinbeck, James Watson, John C. Kendrew. Williams, Crick, and Watson won the award for Physiology or Medicine, and Perutz and Kendrew won for Chemistry.

The Grapes of Wrath, "most serious readers" had stopped reading Steinbeck because of his sentimentality.[6]

Once again, Steinbeck was furious. Yet other writers saw the injustice of these persistent criticisms. American author, Gore Vidal, said critics like Mizener and Alfred Kazin "believe that good literature is written for a small, select group of people like themselves. They could never forgive Steinbeck for saying things that people wanted and needed to hear."[7]

Steinbeck sold his Seventy-Second Street brownstones (which had become burdensome for him) and moved to a very large, luxury apartment in a brand-new building a few blocks away.

Back in the USSR

In the spring of 1963, Steinbeck was asked to join a cultural exchange between America and Russia to help soften their relationship during the Cold War. Previously the poet Robert Frost had participated. Steinbeck asked if he could bring some of the younger contingent of writers, like playwrights Edward Albee and Terrence McNally, the Steinbeck boys' tutor.

In early May, Elaine and John moved back to Sag Harbor, where John suffered a detached retina that nearly blinded him. He spent the whole summer in bed without moving his head, while some of his friends, including the writer John O'Hara, read to him. In September, when he was fully recovered, John and Elaine went to Washington, DC, for a briefing on his trip to Moscow. There, he met with President Kennedy.

In Moscow, the exchange group met up with Edward Albee, who had taken on the role of speaking with dissident Soviet writers. He believed Steinbeck was too imposing a figure and that they would feel more comfortable speaking with someone of their generation.

From September to November, the Steinbecks traveled throughout Russia, meeting up with Albee from time to time. When they arrived in Leningrad on November 8, Steinbeck collapsed and was hospitalized. The doctors determined John was not seriously ill, but exhausted. They recommended three weeks of rest. Steinbeck would not hear of it. Within one day of his release from the hospital, Steinbeck was lecturing at Leningrad State University.

On November 15, the Steinbecks left for Poland. They were in Warsaw on November 22, 1963, when President Kennedy was assassinated. It was a tumultuous time for Steinbeck. He and Elaine flew to Vienna to attend a memorial service. Everywhere they went, people offered their sympathies. They returned to the United States in December and immediately flew to Washington, DC, for a debriefing. Later they had dinner at the White House with the new president, Lyndon Johnson. Lady Bird Johnson and Elaine renewed their acquaintance from their college days at the University of Texas. The Johnsons and the Steinbecks would remain good friends.

Trouble With the Boys

Back in New York for Christmas, John and Elaine finally had time to relax in their new apartment overlooking. Thom and John IV were there, and it was quite a celebration. They saw the boys off at the station to return to school. Everything seemed to be fine until they got a phone call from the school's headmaster. Thom and John IV had not shown up. They were finally found at Gwyn's house, a previously used trick. They complained they could not get close to their father and that he was drunk and always depressed. Terrence McNally noted that John could not get as close to the boys as he wanted to and Gwyn just made it worse by saying awful things about him.

Then Gwyn sued to get more money from John for child support. The boys took Gwyn's side. John wondered if they had even appreciated the trip they had recently taken with him. Elaine and John had to appear in court with Gwyn. The judge awarded Gwyn a very small increase. The judge noted that if John had not been as famous, the hearing would never have been held. Gwyn, severely disappointed, left the courtroom in tears.

That summer, when the boys were visiting, they explained they had to go along with their mother even though they did not want to. John accepted their explanation. According to Elaine, "he loved them very much, but he could not understand their behavior."[8] The gap between the boys and Steinbeck would never be bridged.

The Presidential Medal

In the summer of 1964 Steinbeck learned that he would receive the Presidential Medal of Freedom in a ceremony that September. John spent a lot of time analyzing what he had accomplished in his life at the age of sixty-two. What bothered him the most was that he thought his time had already passed. He noted in a letter to Pat Covici, "More and more, young people look at me in amazement because they thought I was dead."[9] At the award ceremony was Pat Covici, who had a big part, from the beginning, in making this event a reality. It was the last time Pat and John saw each other. Covici died on October 14.

War in Vietnam

Once again, John and Elaine were guests at the White House, where John befriended Jack Valenti, who was an adviser to President Johnson. Johnson continued to seek support from

Steinbeck for the war in Vietnam. Steinbeck was a staunch supporter of Johnson, but not as strong a supporter of the war. After John IV decided to enlist, Steinbeck's support for the war increased. In fact, President Johnson invited John and John IV to the White House in May 1966, for which John was very grateful.

With John IV's enlistment, the war in Vietnam hit closer to home for Steinbeck. He began to look at the war from the perspective of the ordinary soldier who was doing his patriotic duty. He supported the troops, thinking of them as victims, as well as heroes, similar to how he positioned the Joad family in *The Grapes of Wrath*.

While Steinbeck would continue to support President Johnson, his doubts about the war grew, but he stayed quiet. Even after John IV wrote to him that he thought the war was a grave error, Steinbeck continued to remain silent. His personal views on the war would not be made public until after his death. Steinbeck had become sure that the war was a huge mistake.

Harry Guggenheim suggested Steinbeck become a correspondent for *Newsday* with his first-hand observations of Vietnam and the war. Steinbeck was interested. He was particularly keen on going since John IV was there. Elaine would come with him; Steinbeck believed she was indispensable to his well-being.

Steinbeck, accompanied by Major Sam Gipson, got right into the action in Vietnam. He relayed to Harry Guggenheim how the ground war was being fought. Guns and mines were easily hidden in the jungle, and it was tricky to get around. Steinbeck felt as if he were back in his World War II days. He commented that the Viet Cong soldiers who were captured were strong and brave. One night, Steinbeck was allowed to

Steinbeck (right) talks to Marines during his 1966 visit to Vietnam, where he served as a correspondent.

accompany John IV's unit. As John IV relates it, he quickly flew to his combat station, armed with an M-79 grenade. Steinbeck had an M-60 machine gun. "I saw my father behind some sandbags overlooking my position, with his M-60 ready . . . And what an amazing feeling to see him ready in his flack jacket and helmet protecting my back . . . it had been enough to bring us to a brief moment of . . . awareness for each other . . . I felt a brotherly love in my heart."[10]

Steinbeck concluded that most of the soldiers did not want to be there but felt an obligation to their country. Steinbeck did not wish to comment politically; that was as far as he went. John Steinbeck remained loyal to President Johnson and to the country. At this point much of the nation was regretting American involvement in the war. Many felt that Steinbeck had sold out and betrayed his liberal past. *Newsday* cancelled his column.

Failing Health

Steinbeck had covered a great deal of territory in his visit to Vietnam, and by the end of February, when they finally arrived at an air-conditioned hotel, Steinbeck's body gave out. He was in bed for four days. When he felt better, he and Elaine flew to Kyoto to meet up with John IV, who was on leave. All three had a good time. However, when John and Elaine arrived in Tokyo, John was, once again, in agony. He had three crushed discs in his spine, it was discovered, and he was in excruciating pain.

By the time summer rolled around, the Steinbecks were back in Sag Harbor. He was depressed about his pain, about the futility of winning the war in Vietnam, and was frustrated about not letting President Johnson know what he was really thinking.

Steinbeck underwent a back operation that left him extremely weak. All he could do was stay in bed and read. Right before Christmas 1967, John and Elaine flew to Grenada, and rented a cottage where John could recuperate. The sun always had a positive effect on John, and he was sure it would still work for him. They stayed until the end of January and then returned to Sag Harbor. Unfortunately, the Caribbean sun had not worked for John. He continued to feel weak. They had to return to their apartment in the city where the doctors and hospitals were in easy reach.

Along with his medical record sent to Dr. Denton Cox, Steinbeck's physician, John included a note in which he explained that he had no fear of dying, and that he had enjoyed a "good span of life."[11] Steinbeck wanted Dr. Cox to refrain from telling Elaine anything that would cause her pain or sorrow. Steinbeck, it seems, was aware that the last chapter of his life was imminent

John felt miserable in the city. He and Elaine moved back to Sag Harbor. But John suffered another small stroke as well as a minor heart attack. At the request of Dr. Cox, John returned to the city, where he remained in a hospital, under close observation, for three weeks. But as soon as he was released, he insisted on going back to Sag Harbor. He needed to be near the water. In November, John's breathing became more difficult. He was suffering from emphysema and hardening of the arteries.

Last Breaths

Steinbeck had many visitors at home, including Thom and John IV and Elizabeth Otis. One day in 1968 he was reading about a new procedure called a heart bypass. He asked Dr. Cox to send some cardiologists to the apartment to examine him as a possible candidate. When they told him nothing could be done because of his other complications, he apologized for having taken their time.

On the morning of December 20, 1968, Elaine knew John did not have very long to live. Many of his friends visited that day. Elaine slipped into bed with John where they reminisced about the best times they'd had. Elaine fell asleep, and when she woke, John was dead. He took his last breath at 5:30 that afternoon.[12] He died simply, perhaps with some regrets, but surrounded with love. The man who could capture the sound and the heart of ordinary people, who could depict a singular desolate time in America, who had hopes and dreams for his country, who was a journalist, a novelist, a poet and a friend, was silent. His kind would not be heard from again. His ashes are buried in the Hamilton Family Plot, at the Garden of Memories Cemetery of Salinas, California.

STEINBECK'S LEGACY

"I'll be everywhere—wherever you look. Whenever they's a fight so hungry people can eat, I'll be there. Wherever they's a cop beatin' up a guy, I'll be there . . . An' when our folks eat the stuff they raise an' live in the house they build— why I'll be there."

Is Steinbeck's philosophy still valid? It is when one discovers that in the twenty-first century, the Tom Joads of America are still witness to the mistreatment of the oppressed. The farmer, though he may be eating produce he has grown, still declaims that the poor don't have enough food, the disenfranchised suffer the assaults of a corrupt and/or heartless authority, and the blue collar worker has to work at more than one job in order to save enough to meet financial obligations. Our twenty-first century Tom Joads stand helplessly watching our planet choking on atmospheric impurities while those with the power of legislation throughout the planet do little to remedy the planet's plight. Today's Tom Joads see it all. And though they attempt retaliation, so many are whipped back against the fences of intolerance, there is little possibility of being a voice of intelligence or of reason. But Tom Joad remains a powerful voice even if it is of some inconsequence.

Linked Authors

John Steinbeck, William Faulkner, and Ernest Hemingway were keystone authors of the 1960s, linked by their contri-

This statue of Steinbeck stands outside the Salinas library, which is named for him. Despite Steinbeck's rocky relationship with Salinas over the years, the town has come to embrace him once more and stages celebrations each year on his birthday.

butions to American literature. Steinbeck was the youngest. He suffered more slings and arrows than any of the others by scholars, pundits, critics and the press. But his work, without question, resides in the coffers of greatness and has been translated into countless languages throughout the world. He has never been out of print.

As one biographer states, "John Steinbeck remains fresh and relevant to contemporary readers of almost every age and type, raising questions of power and poverty, individualism and community, in warning and in hope."[1] Steinbeck's relevance continues. According to Hollywood's *Variety* magazine, actor James Franco and screenwriter Matt Rager plan to adapt John Steinbeck's 1936 labor-movement novel *In Dubious Battle* as a motion picture that will feature Franco. In a 2014 stage revival of *Of Mice and Men,* co-starring Chris O'Dowd, Franco played George.[2]

Years before, the 1938 Broadway production of the labor-movement play won the New York Drama Critics' Circle Best Play Award. The 1939 film version featured Lon Cheney as Lenny and Burgess Meredith as George, the role that helped make Meredith famous. It also introduced Meredith to Steinbeck, and they became close friends. A thirty-five-year-old actor named Henry Fonda also became Steinbeck's friend following Fonda's now critically acclaimed performance as Tom Joad in the 1940 film adaptation of *The Grapes of Wrath.* Like John Steinbeck, Burgess Meredith, and James Franco, Fonda was a political liberal with progressive social ideas. Like Meredith, he visited Steinbeck in Los Gatos, a twenty-minute drive from Franco's hometown of Palo Alto. Steven Spielberg would produce a remake of *The Grapes of Wrath.* If he doesn't, James Franco might.[3]

Chris O'Dowd and James Franco, stars of the 2014 Broadway adaptation of *Of Mice and Men*, take a bow with the cast on opening night. Steinbeck's legacy is kept alive today through countless stage and film productions of his works.

There's more. Universal Pictures has scheduled production on a film adaptation of *East of Eden* to celebrate the novel's seventy-fifth anniversary. The film will be directed by Tom Hooper from a screenplay by Christopher Hampton. As of now, Jennifer Lawrence has been cast in the role of Cathy Ames. In April 2014, Gary Ross, writer-director of *The Hunger Games*, said that because of its length and changing tone, the film will be split into two.[4]

A New Biography

William Souder, the distinguished, award-winning biographer, will unveil his new biography of John Steinbeck in 2019. Titled *Mad at the World: John Steinbeck and the American Century,* the book will focus on the troubled life of the ecology-driven author. "Steinbeck didn't like school, didn't like Salinas, didn't like working as a reporter in New York. And all of those things didn't like him back."[5]

But Steinbeck was born at the tail end of the Victorian era and died just as America was headed for the moon. It was, for Souder, a perfect slice of American history and a perfect reason to write the new biography. And so, Steinbeck remains as relevant in the twenty-first century as he was in the twentieth.

Chronology

1902– Born February 27 to Olive Hamilton and John Ernst Steinbeck II in Salinas, California, the third of four children.

1915–1919– Attends Salinas High School.

1919–1925– Attends Stanford University, without receiving a degree.

1925– Works as a laborer and as a journalist for the *New York American* in New York City.

1926–1928– Works as a caretaker at a summer home in Lake Tahoe, California.

1929– McBride publishes *Cup of Gold*.

1930– Marries Carol Henning.

1932– *The Pastures of Heaven* is published.

1933– *To a God Unknown* is published.

1934– Mother dies.

1935– *Tortilla Flat* is published.

1936– Father dies.
In Dubious Battle is published.

1937– *Of Mice and Men* and *The Red Pony* are published.
The play *Of Mice and Men* opens in New York.

1938– *Their Blood Is Strong* is published.
The play *Of Mice and Men* is awarded the New York Drama Critics Circle Award.
The Long Valley is published.

1939– *The Grapes of Wrath* is published
The film *Of Mice and Men* is released.

1940– The film *The Grapes of Wrath* is released.
Makes marine expedition in the Gulf of California with Ed Ricketts.
Awarded the National Book Award and the Pulitzer Prize for *The Grapes of Wrath*.

Works on documentary film about living conditions in rural Mexico, *The Forgotten Village*.

1941– *Sea of Cortez* is published.

1942– Divorces Carol.

The Moon Is Down is published.

Bombs Away is published.

The play *The Moon Is Down* opens in New York.

The film *Tortilla Flat* is released.

1943– The film *The Moon Is Down* is released.

Marries Gwyn Conger.

Works as a war correspondent for the *New York Herald Tribune* in Europe and North Africa.

1944– Writes screenplay for Alfred Hitchcock's *Lifeboat*.

First son, Thom, is born on August 2.

1945– *Cannery Row* is published.

1946– Second son, John IV, is born on June 12.

1947– *The Wayward Bus* is published.

The Pearl is published.

Tours Russia with photographer Robert Capa, for the *New York Herald Tribune*.

1948– *A Russian Journal* is published.

Divorces Gwyn.

Elected to American Academy of Arts and Letters.

1950– *Burning Bright* is published.

The play *Burning Bright* opens in New York.

Marries Elaine Anderson Scott.

1951– *The Log from the Sea of Cortez* is published.

1952– The film *Viva Zapata!* is released.

East of Eden is published.

1954– *Sweet Thursday* is published.

1955– *Pipe Dream*, a musical version of *Sweet Thursday*, opens in New York.

1957– *The Short Reign of Pippin IV* is published.

The film *The Wayward Bus* is released.

1958– *Once There Was a War* is published.

1959– Tours England and Wales, researching background for a modern English version of Malory's *Morte d'Arthur*.

1960– Tours United States with his poodle, Charley.

1961– *The Winter of Our Discontent* is published.

1962– *Travels with Charley* is published. Awarded the Nobel Prize for Literature.

1963– Tours Scandinavia, Eastern Europe, and Russia on United States Information Agency cultural mission.

1964– Awarded United States Medal of Freedom by President Lyndon B. Johnson.

1965– Writes articles for *Newsday* from Vietnam.

1966– *America and Americans* is published.

1968– Dies of arteriosclerosis in New York City, December 20.

Chapter Notes

Chapter 1. Living in Salinas

1. John Steinbeck, *East of Eden* (New York: The Viking Press, 1952), 5.
2. Jay Parini, *John Steinbeck, A Biography* (New York: Henry Holt, 1995), 13.
3. Ibid.
4. Ibid., 15.
5. Jackson J. Benson, *The True Adventures of John Steinbeck, Writer* (New York: Penguin, 1984), 21.
6. Ibid.
7. Ibid., 24.
8. Parini, 18.
9. Benson, 58–60.
10. Parini, 35.
11. "American Writers: Steinbeck," *C-SPAN*, http://www.americanwriters.org/classroom/resources /tr_steinbeck.asp. (accessed August 27, 2015).
12. Parini, 42.
13. Thomas Kiernan, *The Intricate Music: A Biography of John Steinbeck* (Boston: Little Brown, 1970), 104–107.
14. Parini, 53–54.
15. Benson, 98–99.
16. Parini, 56–57.
17. Benson, 113.
18. Ibid., 133–134.
19. Parini, 78.

Chapter 2. *Cup of Gold* Gets Published

1. Jackson J. Benson, *The True Adventures of John Steinbeck, Writer* (New York: Penguin Books, 1984), 166.

2. Jay Parini, *John Steinbeck, A Biography* (New York: Henry Holt, 1995), 91–92.

3. Ibid., 98.

4. Thomas Kiernan, *The Intricate Music: A Biography of John Steinbeck* (Boston: Little Brown, 1970), 162.

5. Benson, 219–220.

6. Parini, 124.

7. Benson, 265.

8. Andre Gide, *The Journals of Andre Gide. Vol. IV, 1939–49* (New York: Alfred A. Knopf, 1951), 48.

9. Benson, 324.

10. James Franco, "Group as Character in Steinbeck's *In Dubious Battle*," *Vice*, April 10, 2014, http://www.vice.com/read/group-as-character-in-steinbecks-in-dubious-battle.

Chapter 3. *Of Mice and Men*

1. Herbert N. Foerstel, *Banned in the U.S.A.* (Westport, CT: Greenwood, 2002), 198.

2. Warren French, "End of a Dream," *Steinbeck: A Collection of Critical Essays*, ed. Robert Murray Davis (Englewood Cliffs, NJ: Prentice-Hall, 1972), 64.

3. Ibid., 66.

4. Ibid., 67.

5. Louis Owens, "Of Mice and Men: The Dream of Commitment," *John Steinbeck*, ed. Harold Bloom (New York: Chelsea House, 1987), 146.

6. Marilyn Chandler McEntyre, "Of Mice and Men: A Story of Innocence Retained," *The Betrayal of Brotherhood in the Work of John Steinbeck: Cain Sign*, ed. Michael J. Meyer (Lewiston, NY: Edwin Mellen Press, 2000), 205.

7. John Steinbeck, *Of Mice and Men* (New York: Penguin, 1993), 90.

8. French, 66.

Chapter 4. The World Must Know

1. Charles Wollenberg, "Introduction," The Harvest Gypsies (Berkeley, CA: Heydey Books, 1988), xiii.

2. Jay Parini, *John Steinbeck, A Biography* (New York: Henry Holt, 1995), 180–183.

3. Thomas Kiernan, *The Intricate Music: A Biography of John Steinbeck* (Boston: Little Brown, 1970), 217–218.

4. Jackson J. Benson, *The True Adventures of John Steinbeck, Writer* (New York: Penguin, 1984), 376.

5. "The Red Pony," *Ed Stephan's Front Door,* http://www.ac.wwu.edu/~stephan/Steinbeck/pony.html (December 13, 2003).

6. Benson, 391–392.

7. Parini, 226.

8. Clifton Fadiman, "Highway 66—A Tale of Five Cities," *The New Yorker*, April 15, 1939, 81.

9. Parini, 220.

10. Henry R. Luce, ed., *Time Capsule, 1939* (New York: Time, 1968), 211.

Chapter 5. *The Grapes of Wrath*

1. Peter Lisca, "The Grapes of Wrath," *Steinbeck: A Collection of Critical Essays*, ed. Robert Murray Davis (Englewood Cliffs, NJ: Prentice-Hall, 1972), 93.

2. John Steinbeck, The Grapes of Wrath (New York: Penguin, 1967), 107.

3. Ibid., 449.

4. Ibid., 30

5. Warren French, "The Social Novel at the End of an Era," accessed December 13, 2003, http://ocean.st.usm.edu/~wsimkins/trans.html.

6. Warren French, *John Steinbeck's Fiction Revisited* (Boston: Twayne, 1994), 81.

7. Steinbeck, 537.

8. Lisca, 95.

9. Thomas Kiernan, *The Intricate Music: A Biography of John Steinbeck* (Boston: Little Brown, 1970), 237.

Chapter 6. The Pulitzer Prize

1. Jay Parini, *John Steinbeck, A Biography* (New York: Henry Holt, 1995), 226.

2. Thomas Kiernan, *The Intricate Music: A Biography of John Steinbeck* (Boston: Little Brown, 1970), 243.

3. Ibid., 255.

4. Parini, 265.

5. Jackson J. Benson, *The True Adventures of John Steinbeck, Writer* (New York: Penguin, 1984), 542.

6. Parini, 305.

7. Kiernan, 281.

8. Parini, 315.

9. Benson, 637.

10. Kiernan, 285.

Chapter 7. Troubling Times

1. Thomas Kiernan, *The Intricate Music: A Biography of John Steinbeck* (Boston: Little Brown, 1970), 285.

2. "The Nobel Prize in Literature 1949," Nobelprize.org, http://www.nobelprize.org/nobel_prizes/literature/laureates/1949 (August 27, 2015).

3. Jay Parini, *John Steinbeck, A Biography* (New York: Henry Holt, 1995), 347.

4. John Steinbeck IV and Nancy Steinbeck, *The Other Side of Eden: Life with John Steinbeck* (New York: Prometheus Books, 2001), 80.

5. Pauline Pearson, "East of Eden," *National Steinbeck Center*, June 1995, http://www.steinbeck.org/EastEden.html.

6. Parini, 356.

Chapter 8. *East of Eden*

1. "About John Steinbeck," *Steinbeck Now,* http://www. steinbecknow.com/about-john-steinbeck-2/ (August 27, 2015).
2. John Steinbeck, *East of Eden* (New York: The Viking Press, 1952), 14.
3. Ibid., 263.
4. Bruce Ouderkirk, "Fathers and Sons in *East of Eden,*" *Betrayal of Brotherhood in the Work of John Steinbeck,* ed. Michael J. Meyer (Lewiston, NY: Edwin Mellen Press, 2000), 370.
5. Michael J. Meyer, "Endless Possibilities: The Significance of Nomos in Steinbeck's East of Eden," *The Betrayal of Brotherhood in the Work of John Steinbeck: Cain Sign*, ed. Michael J. Meyer (Lewiston, NY: Edwin Mellen Press, 2000), 427.
6. Richard F. Peterson, "East of Eden," *A Study Guide to Steinbeck*, ed. Tetsumaro Hayashi (Metuchen, NJ: Scarecrow Press, 1974), 74.
7. *East of Eden*, 165.
8. *East of Eden*, 415.
9. Joseph Wood Krutch, "John Steinbeck's Dramatic Tale of Three Generations," *Steinbeck and His Critics, A Record of Twenty-Five Years*, eds. E. W. Tedlock, Jr. and C. V. Wicker (Albuquerque: University of New Mexico Press, 1957), 302.
10. Peterson, 75.
11. Ibid., 76.
12. Ibid., 78–79.
13. *East of Eden*, 132.

Chapter 9. Travels and Politics

1. "John Steinbeck (1902–1968)," 2003, http://www.kirjasto.sci.fi/johnstei.htm.
2. Tim Dirks, "East of Eden (1955)," *The Greatest Films*, http://www.filmsite.org/east.html (accessed August 27, 2015).
3. Jay Parini, *John Steinbeck, A Biography* (New York: Henry Holt, 1995), 361.
4. Ibid., 362.
5. Jackson J. Benson, *The True Adventures of John Steinbeck, Writer* (New York: Penguin, 1984), 754.
6. Parini, 385.
7. Warren French, "The Social Novel at the End of an Era," http://ocean.st.usm.edu/~wsimkins/trans.html (accessed December 13, 2003).
8. Parini, 401.
9. Ibid., 409.
10. Elia Kazan, *Elia Kazan: A Life* (New York: Doubleday, 1989), 786.
11. Parini, 420.
12. Ibid., 420–421.
13. Parini, 434.

Chapter 10. The Nobel Prize

1. Jay Parini, *John Steinbeck, A Biography* (New York: Henry Holt, 1995), 442.
2. Ibid.
3. Parini, 444.
4. Ibid., 445.
5. Warren French, "The Social Novel At the End of An Era," http://ocean.st.usm.edu/~wsimkins/trans.html (accessed December 13, 2003).
6. Parini, 448.

7. Ibid., 449.

8. Ibid., 457.

9. Ibid., 458.

10. John Steinbeck IV and Nancy Steinbeck, *The Other Side of Eden: Life with John Steinbeck* (New York: Prometheus Books, 2001), 106.

11. Parini, 479.

12. Jackson J. Benson, *The True Adventures of John Steinbeck, Writer* (New York: Penguin, 1984), 1036.

Chapter 11. Steinbeck's Legacy

1. "About John Steinbeck," *Steinbeck Now* http://www.steinbecknow.com/about-john-steinbeck-2/ (accessed August 27, 2015).

2. James Franco, "James Franco Writes About Motion Picture Adaptation of Steinbeck's *In Dubious Battle*," *Steinbeck Now*, June 24, 2015, http://www.steinbecknow.com/2015/06/03/james-franco-motion-picture-in-dubious-battle/.

3. Dave Trumbore, "Steven Spielberg to Produce The Grapes of Wrath Remake for Dreamworks," Collider, July 2, 2013, http://collider.com/the-grapes-of-wrath-steven-spielberg/.

4. Tim Appelo, "Jennifer Lawrence's 'East of Eden' May Be Two Movies, Says Director," *Hollywood Reporter*, April 12, 2014, http://www.hollywoodreporter.com/news/jennifer-lawrences-east-eden-may-695666.

5. William Ray, "Pulitzer Prize Finalist Writing John Steinbeck Biography: Talk with William Souder," *Steinbeck Now*, June 19, 2015, http://www.steinbecknow.com/2015/05/27/pulitzer-prize-john-steinbeck-biography-william-souder/.

Literary Terms

allegory—A symbolic representation or expression.

foreshadow—To hint at something that will happen later in a story.

intercalary—Something inserted between two things or parts.

irony—The use of words to express an idea that is opposite to the words' literal meaning.

metaphor—A figure of speech in which a comparison is made between two words or phrases that have no literal relationship.

personification—A figure of speech in which an inanimate object is treated as, or compared to, a living thing.

phalanx—An organized group of people.

protest novel—A novel with a message about a current social or political condition and calls for change.

symbol—Something that stands for, represents, or suggests another thing.

theme—A distinctive quality or concern in one or more works of fiction.

transcendentalism—A philosophical movement that taught that man was basically good and that human life went beyond the experiences of the physical world.

Major Works by
John Steinbeck

Cup of Gold (1929)
The Pastures of Heaven (1932)
To a God Unknown (1933)
Tortilla Flat (1935)
In Dubious Battle (1936)
Of Mice and Men (1937)
The Red Pony (1937)
The Long Valley (1938)
The Grapes of Wrath (1939)
The Forgotten Village (1941)
Sea of Cortez (1941)
The Moon Is Down (1942)
Bombs Away (1942)
The Portable Steinbeck (1943)
Cannery Row (1945)
The Pearl (1947)
The Wayward Bus (1947)
A Russian Journal (1948)
Burning Bright (1950)
The Log from the Sea of Cortez (1951)
East of Eden (1952)
Sweet Thursday (1954)
Pipe Dream (1956)
The Short Reign of Pippin IV (1957)
Once There Was a War (1958)
The Winter of Our Discontent (1961)
Travels with Charley (1962)
America and Americans (1966)

Journal of a Novel: The East of Eden *Letters* (1969)
A Life in Letters (1975)
Viva Zapata! (1975)
Acts of King Arthur and His Noble Nights (1976)
Letters to Elizabeth (1978)
Uncollected Stories of John Steinbeck (1986)
Selected Essays of John Steinbeck (1987)
The Harvest Gypsies (1988)
Working Days (1989)

Movies for Theatrical Showing

Of Mice and Men (1939)
The Grapes of Wrath (1940)
The Forgotten Village (1941)
Tortilla Flat (1942)
The Moon Is Down (1943)
Lifeboat (1944)
A Medal for Benny (1945)
The Pearl (1947)
The Red Pony (1949)
Viva Zapata! (1952)
East of Eden (1955)
The Wayward Bus (1957)
Flight (1961)
Cannery Row (1982)
Of Mice and Men (1992)

Movies for Television

Molly Morgan (1950)
O'Henry's Full House (1952)

Nobody's Fool (1954)
Nothing So Monstrous (1954)
The House (1954)
A Medal for Benny (1954)
The Flight (1956)
America and Americans (1967)
Of Mice and Men (1968)
Travels with Charley (1968)
The Harness (1972)
The Red Pony (1973)

FURTHER READING

Bloom, Harold, ed. *John Steinbeck*. Broomall, PA: Chelsea House, 1999.

Buzbee, Lewis. *Steinbeck's Ghost*. New York: Square Fish, 2010.

Ferrell, Keith. *John Steinbeck: The Voice of the Land*. Lanham, MD: M. Evans & Co., 2014.

Haugen, Hayley Mitchell, ed. *The American Dream in John Steinbeck's Of Mice and Men*. San Diego: Greenhaven Press, 2010.

Morretta, Alison. *John Steinbeck and the Great Depression*. New York: Cavendish Square, 2014.

INTERNET ADDRESSES

National Steinbeck Center

www.steinbeck.org/

Contains a comprehensive catalogue of Steinbeck's work in addition to information about his life and most famous novels.

The Center for Steinbeck Studies

www2.sjsu.edu/steinbeck/

Provides biography, photos, and videos as well as news and text of Steinbeck's Nobel Prize speech.

Steinbeck Now

www.steinbecknow.com

Learn about Steinbeck's life, books, films, music, and his beliefs from ecology to politics.

Index